David E. Stanley
David Gruder, PhD

Conversations with the King

Journals of a Young Apprentice

EPIPHANY
NOW
PUBLISHING

EPIPHANY NOW PUBLISHING, SAN DIEGO, CALIFORNIA

ISBN: 978-0-578-10262-7

Printed in the United States of America

TO KATY...

YOUR LOVE HAS TRANSFORMED MY LIFE

ELVIS & DAVID ~ 1967

CONTENTS

"Transparency is the essence of Authenticity."

~ David E. Stanley

ACKNOWLEDGEMENTS

I am in gratitude always to the special and talented individuals that have been a huge part of my personal spiritual journey and who have helped to make this book possible.

Elvis Presley: You were the Master that took me on as a young apprentice. You left me a legacy and a message that goes out to the world in this literary work. I love you... the conversations continue.

Dr. David Gruder: My friend, you helped me peel back the layers of my inner self and put them into the words that filled the pages of this book.

BJ Dohrmann: You set the example of what real cooperation in the corporate world can be. You opened the door to a new way of life by providing a haven where dreams can and do come true. You encourage me by nurturing my God-given gifts.

Eve Hogan: You are that special soul who led me to the Labyrinth and met me when I came out. The miracle continues.

Dr. Richard Kaye: You are the one I first discussed the miracles and messages of this book with, back in 2005. You have been with me ever since supporting my journey and quietly making sure that message never died.

IN DEEP APPRECIATION

David M. Corbin/Dean Parks/Tri Ma Gia/JulieAnn Engel

Lauren E. Miller/Dean Fulford/James M. Blakemore/Patrick S. Durkin

David Wallace/Allen Taylor/Kimberly A. Kunasek/Nadine Lajoie

Marie Hue Nguyen/Heidi Fischer/Michal Mael/Paul Fischer

James T. Niemeyer/Craig Newell/Dennis Gauba/Linda Fischer

~

SPECIAL THANKS TO

Chris Collins/ Laura Rubinstein/Tom Jurgensen/Maria Speth

Lauren Solomon/Bob LaBine/Laurie Morse Gruder

Larry Geller/Roger Anthony

Ken Rutt/Samar Waterworth/Johanna Gratz/Laura Rutt

PREFACE

"Are you satisfied with the image you've established?" a reporter asked Elvis Presley during a press conference in New York City in June of 1972. We were there for a series of concerts he was doing at Madison Square Garden.

Elvis replied, "Well, the image is one thing, and a human being is another, you know. So, it's very hard to live up to an image. I'll put it that way."

Elvis never told the press or the public who he was as a human being. His privacy was all that preserved his ultimately unsuccessful efforts to hold onto what remained of his authentic self.

Five years later, I was among the first to discover Elvis's lifeless body in the mansion that he had lovingly and selflessly shared with me since

1960. I had arrived at Graceland as a four-year-old boy, along with my two brothers and my mother. My mother had just become the new wife of Elvis's widowed father, Vernon Presley.

When I met him, I knew nothing of Elvis the icon. To me, he was simply my new big brother. I felt an instant love from this total stranger that went far deeper than anything I had experienced in my young life. His embrace felt complete and unconditional.

From the beginning, Elvis always referred to me as his brother. But, he became far more to me than the new big brother of an emotionally confused young boy. Over time he became my father figure, mentor, spiritual advisor, and ultimately, my boss. In June of 1972, two months before I turned seventeen and after having grown up with him at Graceland for twelve years, I was one of his full-time personal aides when he talked at the New York press conference about his public image and private self.

Just weeks after I had begun traveling with him full-time, Elvis took me aside at his Beverly Hills home for what would become one of our many private conversations. He was wearing an ankh around his neck that he often wore. It contained a beautiful black onyx. (The ankh is the ancient Egyptian symbol for eternal life.) Noticing that I was admiring it, he excused himself for a moment. When he returned, he held another ankh in his hands. As the master told his young apprentice about the meditation he wanted me to start doing, he presented me with this ankh, inviting me to wear it as a symbol of our spiritual bond.

Although I was aware of the icon, I knew the man. A man the public never knew. A man who was galaxies different from his public persona. A man who the masses remain mesmerized by to this day; for reasons that go far beyond who the icon appeared to be.

During our private conversations Elvis expressed things to me that he never shared with the press, the public, or the vast majority of those with whom he was closest. Now, it is time to lift the veil on those conversations.

This book is about the extraordinary lessons that Elvis the private mystic and healer taught me during my seventeen years as his young apprentice. It is also about the equally important lessons I learned from witnessing his titanic struggle between his most authentic spiritual self, his private demons, and his feeling imprisoned by the public icon he had become.

This is the one Elvis story that has never been written because I'm the only one who could tell it. Only now do I at last understand that story well enough to share it in ways that will be healing to many, perhaps including you.

Why does Elvis continue to hold sway with millions around the world for reasons they don't understand, even thirty-four years after his death? *Conversations with the King: Journals of a Young Apprentice* is your doorway into the secrets behind that mystery. This book gives you never-before-available access to the wisdom and gifts Elvis never openly discussed in public. The untold stories each chapter contains revolve around a life lesson that invites you into discovering your answers to the mysteries of your life.

At the end of each chapter you will find questions about these lessons that you might find valuable to ponder.

Whether you've been touched by Elvis or not, you'll be enthralled by the lessons this book illuminates. They are for all who seek to become more authentic, wise, and enduringly happy.

These lessons transformed my life. I believe that Elvis Presley, the mystic and healer, passed them on to me for reasons that go far beyond my personal growth and spiritual development. Through my journey from apprentice to master, it became clear that my mission is to bring these lessons to you. My heartfelt wish is that you find them to be as beneficial throughout your spiritual journey as they continue to be on mine.

INTRODUCTION

As I drove up the driveway to Graceland with my family, it was very much different than it had been fifty-one years before, when I was just a four-year-old boy. A sense of wonder was no longer there. The hope of acceptance wasn't an issue. Driving through the gates of the Graceland Mansion during Elvis Week of 2011, with thousands of fans there from all over the world for their annual pilgrimage, felt unfamiliar.

Though I have been to Graceland many times since his passing, something was very different: *I was different.*

As I strolled the grounds of my old home, along with my wife Katy, and stepdaughter Mya, I noticed that we were being accompanied by dragonflies.

In that moment we couldn't help but recall the dragonflies that had been showing up in many unexpected moments during the writing of this book, and especially in the weeks prior to our visit to Memphis.

I particularly recalled the stunning red dragonfly that spent the day with Dr. Gruder and me in his garden at his home in San Diego as we were writing one day.

Katy would later inform me about the symbolic significance of the dragonfly. It apparently is recognized around the world as a symbol of change and specifically in relation to self-realization, which includes mental and emotional maturity and embracing life's deeper meaning.

Upon entering the Meditation Gardens, Elvis's final resting place, the number of dragonflies intensified into the hundreds. They were literally swarming above our heads.

Katy took my hand and said, "Look, David, look at all the dragonflies!!"

Approaching the grave, everyone's mood shifted, including that of my brother, Billy, and his wife, Monica. All appeared to be suffering from a sense of loss... except for Katy and me. We found ourselves more in gratitude than in mourning. As I stood, silently communicating with my famed master, my conversation was intuitively interrupted by Katy, who said, "David, did you hear that? Did you hear what he said? Did you get your validation?"

"I did," I answered.

I was no longer the apprentice. I was now the teacher.

In that moment, I was flooded with an awareness of the surprising way that I had lived my life, far more in Elvis's image than I had realized. This revelation was more powerful because of the transformation that had begun months before. Now it was confirmed. Now I understood more than ever the unspoken meaning behind why people all over the world still love Elvis all these decades after his death.

Many have struggled to put into words why Elvis continues to have such sway over their hearts. For example, we ran into Linda Moore, who has never missed an Elvis week in the thirty-four years since his death. I asked her, "What do you love the most about Elvis?"

Her answer was simple and clear. "His soul, David. His soul." She then added, "Understand, David, I don't have him, he has me."

Just the week before, Katy and I, while on a business trip in Las Vegas, dropped in to an Elvis Tribute Artists' convention at the Hilton, where Elvis performed twice a year throughout the seventies. I got into a conversation with a fan, and asked her, "What do you love most about Elvis?" Her response was the same.

"His soul. He could have been a postman, a milkman, or selling phone books. I still would have loved him. It is his soul."

There was a time during my spiritual journey when I would have considered this seemingly over-the-top adoration the most outrageous act of idolatry I had ever seen. No longer. At Elvis's graveside, I received full confirmation about what his fans felt so deeply and yet had so much difficulty putting into words.

Elvis was a prototype of spiritual transformation in the modern age. The twentieth century marked the end of enlightenment only being available to monks in monasteries. Suddenly, secret spiritual wisdom was becoming available to the masses. The problem was that the public had no template for how to step into this. Neither did spiritual elders, political leaders, or entertainers.

Elvis did. He was far more than the prototype of the rock star and entertainer. He was the model of a newly emerging path of spiritual struggling and development. He was the personification of the challenges of coming out of the spiritual closet that many millions of people have been dealing with. His life embodied the journey all of us take as we try to reconcile living our deepest spiritual wisdom with the expectations of the people around us.

I was blessed to privately witness and experience the profound gifts that Elvis kept from the public eye, as well as his dark struggles to bridge the gulf between his extraordinary spiritual awareness and his very human challenges that were magnified by his icon status.

In our earthly life we have jobs, careers, family, and other obligations and expectations. This calls us to create strong individual personalities. Society's collective consciousness is much grounded in survival, appearance, and material gain. In contrast, the measuring stick of the mystic is our beingness, of never losing connection with our essence, which is the blend of our authentic self with our unity with all. The inner split that these two sets of priorities commonly create can cause the greatest of people to lose their way.

I know because after Elvis died I lost my way, too. But I always continued to feel his presence and to know that I had an unmet calling in my life. That calling came from the most authentic spiritual side of me. But, it was crowded out during the period of my life that I spent focused on worldly survival.

All of this began to change in June of 2010. The Bible, in Matthew 7:7 it says, "Knock and the door shall be opened to you; seek and you shall find." What people often don't understand is that frequently those answers come in the most unlikely of ways.

My first answer came in the form of an intuitive healer who lovingly slipped past my barriers to gain my trust. My second came in the form of a psychologist who happened to be an integrity expert. As unlikely as it is, this ex rock-and-roller and former evangelist bonded with the intuitive spiritual healer and the integrity-driven shrink.

What you're about to read is what has come out of this unlikely collaboration. It has finally integrated my seventeen years as Elvis's apprentice, the life experiences I had following his death, and the subsequent transformation that enabled me to see why Elvis continues to have such a huge impact, not only on my life but the world's as well.

Elvis once said that if his spiritual quest could reach just one life then it would have been worth it. For me, if this book can reach just one person it will be worth it. My prayer is that reading this will help you embody the greatness of your authentic spiritual self in the fabric of your everyday life.

ELVIS & DAVID ~ 1977

CHAPTER ONE

THE LAST CONVERSATION

"David, who am I?" Although Elvis had asked me this question many times over the years, on this day he asked it with such a strong a sense of urgency that it rattled me.

"You're 'The King'," I answered, trying not to show how I felt.

Elvis lifted his Bible in his right hand, saying, "David, there is only one King. Come sit with me." So began my final conversation with the king.

It was August 14, 1977. Elvis was sitting on his bed in his Graceland mansion reading the Bible, as he so often did. The effects of years of prescribed medication abuse had turned him from the once gorgeous sex symbol millions had adored into an isolated, lonely, shell of a man.

"Gosh, a lot's happened over the year."

"Yeah, Boss, it has."

We spent a few minutes talking about some challenges going on in our family. He was concerned about his dad's impending divorce from my mother. He wondered how I was feeling about it and wanted to assure me that this would not affect our relationship.

"What do you think about Daddy and Dee?"

"I don't. Ain't none of my business, Boss. I'm with you all the way."

Elvis had been far more of a parent to me than my mom, my dad, or even my stepfather, Vernon. My loyalty was to him.

However, that's not what Elvis most wanted this conversation to be about. He stood up, and I followed his lead. He then brought me fully into his arms, saying, "I love you, David."

I responded with, "I love you, too." My emotions brought me back to Elvis's hug seventeen years earlier, when he first welcomed me into his family. Today's heartfelt embrace, two weeks shy of my 22nd birthday, felt eerily like that first one.

As we broke from our embrace we stood face-to-face, man-to-man. "Listen," said Elvis, "I want you to know something. The next time you see me I'm going to be in a different place, on a higher plane."

Puzzled by his words, I glanced at the stacks of books on spirituality and personal development that were next to his bed. They accompanied him wherever he went, along with his Bible. I figured he was quoting from one of them.

"No, Boss," I fumbled, "the next plane is going to be yours on the 16th." We were scheduled to leave in two days on his next concert tour, which was to begin in Portland, Maine. He dismissed my response, sat back down on the bed, and returned to his reading.

I moved toward the door and looked back at him, haunted by his profound words. "Hey, Boss...."

"The 16th, David," he interrupted before I could complete my unformed thought, "the 16th."

With that, I left his bedroom, closing his door behind me, not yet knowing that I had just closed the door on a chapter of my life.

When Elvis said what would turn out to be his final words to me, he had for years lived as though a prisoner in solitary confinement. He had become suffocated by the expectations that the iconic public self demanded, which stood in stark contradiction to both his light and dark private selves. His dark, self-destructive private self exerted ever-increasing domination as he approached his appointment with death.

Even so, all the way through his final conversation with me, he had never stopped yearning to find—and live his life from—his authentic, higher self. "David, who am I?" rings in my ears to this day. Not only as *his* question to me, but for many years as *my* question to myself.

"It's not that I'm not liked; it's that I'm misunderstood." ~ Elvis Presley

What most people didn't understand about Elvis is that he had three distinctly different selves. The first was his public self: his carefully created icon status. The second was his extraordinary spiritually authentic seeker, who few knew about or understood. And the third was his equally private self-destructive side that ultimately led to his death.

> *"There are too many people that depend on me. I'm too obligated.*
> *I'm in too far to get out." ~ Elvis Presley*

On August 16, 1977, my friend Mark and I drove through the Graceland gates. I had some free time before we needed to prepare Elvis for our departure later that evening to Portland, Maine.

Mark asked me, "Is Elvis here now?" So powerful was Elvis's presence, and so deep was my intuitive connection with him that I could feel when we were in the same building.

I felt unsettled, just as I had been two days before. "No he's not," I reluctantly replied, knowing full well that I was saying the opposite of what I had every reason to believe was true.

Something definitely wasn't right, but I didn't know what to make of my feeling. I had not yet developed a trust in my intuition when it didn't match what my head knew. It would be many years before I would accept that even had I trusted my intuition that day, it would not have changed the outcome.

Mark and I went downstairs and began shooting pool. Moments later, Amber, the niece of Ginger Alden, Elvis's current girlfriend, entered the room.

"David, Elvis is sick. He's asleep on the bathroom floor and won't wake up."

Having seen him in this state many times over the prior several years, I assumed he had once again taken too much medication and that he would ultimately sleep it off. I also knew that this news would probably mean that we would need to make arrangements to cancel his upcoming concert tour. Knowing from Amber that others were already tending to Elvis, my first task was to get Mark off the premises immediately.

I whisked him home. As I raced back to the Graceland gates not five minutes after having left, an ambulance was entering from the opposite direction. My heart dropped; although I also knew that standard operating procedure was that if a concert needed to be cancelled, Elvis needed to go to the hospital to verify that the cancellation was legitimate.

Following the ambulance as it proceeded to the front of the house, I saw Elvis's cousin, Patsy Gamble, running out the front door screaming hysterically. That was the first moment I realized this situation could be quite different from all the others I'd been through with Elvis over the years. I thought to myself, "This could be serious."

I took the driveway to the back. Jumping out of the car, I raced through the house, up the steps, and into Elvis's bathroom.

There I saw the sight that has since haunted me. Elvis was lying unconscious in a fetal position. Charlie Hodge and Joe Esposito along with Al Strada hovered over him. Moments after I arrived, they rolled Elvis over onto his back. His face and chest were blue and bloated. His black tongue was vice-gripped by his clenched teeth.

I moved toward his body at the exact moment the ambulance attendants burst into the bathroom. They immediately began frantic efforts to try to revive him. But, "too late" had arrived long before any of *us* had.

Vernon, my stepfather, who was beside Elvis, was moaning, "My son is dead. My son is dead." His mistress Sandy, a nurse, was making every effort to keep him calm. Suddenly he took my hand, placed it on Elvis's leg, and looked right through me with tears steaming down his face. "Feel him, David. He's cold. My son is dead."

All I felt in that moment, other than shock, was anger. "Why would Elvis do this to me? Had he said goodbye two days before even though I hadn't realized it? Was his death premeditated? Or was it a heart attack like the autopsy would later claim?"

Those answers didn't matter to me. All that mattered in that moment was that my best friend, father figure, and spiritual mentor—the only person I had ever felt truly loved me, and who I had allowed myself to fully love and trust—had left me.

We picked up his body and placed it on the gurney. A paramedic and I had him by his shoulders, and Joe, Al, and the other paramedic by his legs. We moved his lifeless body out the front door to the waiting ambulance. Charlie, Al, and Joe jumped in the back. At that moment, Dr. George Nichopoulos, Elvis's personal physician (we called him Dr. Nick) pulled up in his car and immediately transferred into the ambulance as well. It raced off for the hospital, along with seventeen years of my life.

It was all so surreal. Undoubtedly the darkest day I have ever experienced. Soon after, I was in my car along with another one of Elvis's cousins, Billy Smith, speeding toward Baptist Memorial Hospital in downtown Memphis. When we arrived, we saw that nearby the empty ambulance, a small crowd of fans and the media had already begun to gather at the hospital's emergency room entrance.

Billy and I sprinted inside. We were immediately taken to a waiting room beside the one in which the emergency room doctors were frantically making last ditch attempts to revive Elvis.

Moments after we arrived, Dr. Nick entered the waiting room. He told Joe, Al, Charlie, Billy, and I that Elvis was officially dead.

Our heads dropped. Our eyes filled with tears. We embraced each other. It was the saddest day of my life.

Our first moments of grief were interrupted by Dr. Nick when he informed Joe that we needed to hold a press conference. I couldn't bear to be there for that. I left the waiting room, walked out of the hospital where the crowds had grown even bigger, and somehow found my way to my car. Driving home, I turned on the radio only to hear the official announcement that Elvis Aaron Presley was dead.

The world lost a king that day but I lost much more than that. I lost a big brother. My anger and shock at last began to melt into tears. I pulled the car over to the side of the road and wept.

"Do not stand at my grave and cry. I'm not there and didn't die."
~ Elvis Presley

August 17, 1977. It was just a day after Elvis had died, but already the mailbags were stacked high with letters from all over the world. Flowers covered the fourteen acres that Graceland rested upon. Helicopters filled the sky to get the best shots of the massive carpet of color that Elvis's fans had created. An estimated 100,000 mourners flocked through the Graceland foyer to pay their final respects to their fallen king.

The next day, it was the family's turn. As I approached the open casket that housed his body, my mind was focused on something Elvis had always told me: "In death we shed our body for something beyond it." As I looked upon what remained of the physical Elvis, I felt for the first time in my young life the truth of what he had taught me.

In that moment, however, that truth was true but not useful; the lifeless empty shell he had occupied was still my closest link to him. I took his hands, laid my head on his chest, and said, "I miss you. I love you." And then, reverting back to the anger I felt alongside my grief, I inwardly screamed at him, "Why did you leave me like this?!"

But, instead of a conversation, this was in fact a monologue; one in which, for the first time, he did not respond.

It was awhile before I came to realize that our conversations had in fact not ended; Elvis's death would ultimately become a monumental wakeup call on my road to spiritual awakening.

Sadly for Elvis, the only way he could be free to fully step into his authentic self was from the other side. He left me behind with this unsolved puzzle: the puzzle of how to achieve this during life. Solving this mystery has taken me decades of extraordinary experiences, massive mistakes, and angels gradually opening my eyes. Elvis was the first of those angels and although I didn't know it at the time, others were on the way.

Questions to Ponder…

- We all have our own version of the three selves Elvis had: 1) The self we want to be known as by others; 2) The insecure and sometimes toxic self-defeating self we try to only show behind closed doors, if at all; and 3) Our wise, loving, and light-filled authentic self, who we share with only a few, or we fully shield from view. Write a description of the qualities of each of your three selves.

- How often have you talked yourself out of your intuition because it seemed to contradict what you thought you knew? When have you wished you would have inquired further when someone told you something that startled you? Write a commitment statement to yourself about how you will practice trusting your intuition more.

- Who have your angels been? How long after they had come and gone did it take you to fully appreciate the angels they were and the lessons they brought into your life to teach you? What were those lessons? Consider being more attentive to the angels who are currently in your life, and the gifts they're trying to offer you.

CHAPTER TWO

THE FIRST CONVERSATION

Fate, not bloodlines or choice, made me part of rock & roll's first family. My mother had left my father to marry Vernon Presley, whom she met in Germany, where Elvis was stationed at the time.

It was February, 1960 when Vernon moved Mom, my two brothers, and me into Graceland, Elvis's home in Memphis, Tennessee. Elvis returned a month later.

The day I met him, I had no idea who he was, and I was far too young to have the vaguest concept of what a rock star was. All I knew was what I felt the moment he scooped me up in his arms, gave me a hug, and said, "Welcome to my family."

A deep feeling of acceptance, healing, and safety entered my life for the very first time. Gone was the inadequacy and shame I had felt over wearing corrective shoes and braces to fix the clubfoot I was born with. Gone were my feelings of having been taken away from my biological father. Gone was my confusion and fear about whether I had a place in this world.

That moment changed my life forever. I, of course, didn't know it then but this was the beginning of my spiritual journey. Elvis's hug, touch, smile, and charm lit me up. It was decades before I would experience that kind of wholehearted embrace from anyone else. Or allow anyone to show me as much love as he did.

Thus was the beginning of my fishbowl existence. You've heard the expression, "What happens in Vegas stays in Vegas?" I learned young that what happens in Graceland stays in Graceland. I learned that loyalty meant isolation; I was never to talk to others about private life in the Presley family, or to open up to others about my emotions and inner world. That's how private of a life I had suddenly and involuntarily entered.

Even inside the family there was only so much that was allowed to be discussed. Except with Elvis. He would become my teacher and every day would become a lesson. From music to sports, and, unbeknownst to me as a child, the gifts of the spirit.

My early years at Graceland set the stage for the deep spiritual conflicts I would struggle with as an adult. As a young boy, I was shown two profoundly contradictory forms of the life of the spirit: my mother's and Elvis's.

My mother was a devoted member of the Church of Christ. At that time, this denomination revolved around rigid rules and the fear of hell. Things like having long hair, listening to the "wrong" kind of music, and boys swimming with girls, were sentences to eternal damnation.

The Church of Christ believed in singing, but they didn't believe in organs or pianos, let alone guitars, basses, and drums. They took the Scripture from the Book of Ephesians (5:19), "Singing and making melody in your heart to the Lord," literally. Making or listening to instrumental music was considered sinful. I even remember playing "Jesus Christ Superstar" at home and my mother was calling the deacons because she was worried that "the devil's music" had gotten a hold of me.

Over the years, her beliefs would eventually soften. But, the initial contrast between her original convictions and the world of rock-and-roll that I'd entered was unfathomable to me. Was Elvis a spiritual inspiration or a ticket to hell? For me, the answer was easy. My allegiance was with him.

Despite the contradiction, Elvis strongly encouraged me to go to church with my mother, just as he had done with his. Although he had developed his musical chops singing in church, he no longer went. He felt he was called to minister the gospel through music. His church was playing this music at home and in concert halls. In fact, the only Grammys he ever received were from his gospel albums. Hearing his gospel music ring through Graceland, and sitting in front of him on the music room floor drinking it in, reached my heart in ways that going to church never did. Yet, according to many denominations, Elvis was lost because he didn't go to church—their church.

Through Elvis's gospel music I first felt the presence of the spirit as a young boy. This Elvis that I knew during my early years with him was a good man. He didn't smoke or drink, and I wasn't yet exposed to his world of women, or the other vices that would later plague his life.

In contrast to my mother's highly judgmental and fear-based church, Elvis showed me a version of spirit that was nonjudgmental and nourishing. One day in church, a deacon said to me in front of the congregation, "If you don't get your hair cut you're going to hell." The young child I was thought, "If I'm bad, what's Elvis? If I'm going to hell isn't Elvis going there, too?"

His gentleness and healing touch taught me about God's love in ways that the fear of hell never could. While denominational fear-based rules and rigid dogma turned me off, Elvis's belief in me and his ongoing encouragement awakened my teachable spirit.

However, gifts of the spirit, for me, meant one big contradiction. I had no idea as a child how to reconcile this. I felt on some level like I needed to choose one over the other.

Not knowing how to put this conflict into words, let alone who to talk to about it, my inner struggle took the form of outward rebellion. I remember the day I was kicked out of the Christian school my mother had enrolled me in. I was big for my age. Between my size and all the energy I had my legs kept hitting my desk. This annoyed my teacher to the point where she grabbed me by the ear and pulled me into the hall. It wasn't a minute later when she was lying on the floor as a result of my right hook. Much to my mother's disappointment, I was thrown out. She tried to help me by sending me to a psychiatrist. His solution was to put me on Ritalin.

I grew up not knowing the difference between love and fear. My fear of God stifled my heart. My love of spirit got me in trouble. The aspect of love I did plug into from my mother's spiritual influence was Christ loving us by dying for us. The love of God that Elvis showed me inspired me and set me on my spiritual journey.

In my first years at Graceland, I now realize I had begun to develop a similar split in me to the one Elvis had. He activated a part of me that was all about teachability, love, and exploration. Yet, an inner war had also begun that continued to tear me apart until literally months before I started writing this book.

By the time I was twelve my relationship with Christ was more out of stark raving fear than love, illumination, and grace. I accepted Christ as my Savior during a crusade at the Mid-South Coliseum in Memphis, Tennessee. I really didn't feel any different afterward. This public profession of faith followed by baptism was merely my attempt to relieve the fear that had been instilled in me through my mother's church leaders.

Looking back on those years, I realize the profound impact that denominational ideologies and methodologies can have on a young mind. I understand the Scripture that says, "You will come to me as a child or not at all." But, I feel that too many denominations still abuse this by indoctrinating individuals into rigid regulations rather than allowing them to personally experience the mercy, grace, and illumination of God's love.

Although, I believe that denominations have their place in this world. To this day I embrace the teachings of Christ. I also believe the part of the Bible where Paul says, "Work out your own salvation." God speaks to us in many different ways. It's the authenticity of how He speaks to you directly that I feel is the true essence of His love, grace, and mercy.

The question is not, "What do you believe?" The question is, "Why do you believe?"

How did you come to your fundamental core beliefs? Were they something you were taught as a child? Were they driven by fear? Do you find yourself asking whether there is more? The only way these questions can be answered is in the guidance Paul provided: work out your own salvation. Go with that inner-self, authenticity, and conviction.

Let me encourage you to listen to those angels who have inspired you. For me, it was an unlikely one: Elvis Presley. For you, it could have been a former spouse or significant other. It could have been through a song or a film, or even a needy person you gave money to on a street corner. Or perhaps it was through "new thought" teachers like Deepak Chopra, Dr. Wayne Dyer, or Eckhart Tolle.

Whoever your angels were and are they were sent for a reason. That reason was to awaken you to your authentic self.

We've all had teachers from whom we've learned characteristics of the three selves introduced in the previous chapter: our public self, our private dark self, and our authentic self. In my world at that time, there was the authentic self of Elvis Presley, the one I dearly loved and who set me on my spiritual path. But, he also, like the rest of us, had a dark private self. One that was hidden from his fans and the rest of this world as a result of his massive iconic public self.

As you read what I'm about to say, please remember that I in no way seek to attack Elvis. I loved him very much. I merely point out the fact that he had a dark private self, a public self, and an authentic self. I instead want his mistakes to help save others from making similar ones, just as they have done for me.

Even though Elvis was a loving, caring man, there was also an Elvis who had a temper that all of us in the Presley family and inner circle knew better than to activate. There was an Elvis whose marriage fell apart as a result of his infidelity. And there was an Elvis who once flew to Washington, D.C., to privately meet with President Nixon about the negative influences that he felt John Lennon was having on youth through advocating drug use. Yet, massive amounts of prescription drugs contributed to his death.

I personally believe that Elvis's inability to reconcile his three selves is part of what killed him. His private authentic self was so often drowned out by his private ugly self, and so often overshadowed by his public icon self, that this is why I now feel he kept asking me, "David, who am I?"

All of us deal with this challenge in one form or another. We build a public self—the person we want others to see us as. We hide the self we believe people would dislike or disapprove of, and usually because they would! And the more the gap grows between our public and dark private selves, the dimmer our genuine authentic light gets. Until, as in Elvis's case, it becomes snuffed out. This became the challenge in my own life for many years. While Elvis's spiritual influence set me on the illuminated path, it was the other two elements that Elvis instilled in me that I needed to overcome in order to fully travel that path.

This is the real tragedy of Elvis's life. If he had found a way to put his private dark self to rest, and become un-imprisoned by his public iconic self, I believe he would still be with us. Part of how I honor him is that I approach each day as an opportunity to further solve in my own life this puzzle that remained unsolved in him.

How about you? How aware are you of your three selves? Who taught you, whether they meant to or not, what your public self should appear to be, and the qualities it was supposed to have? Who was it that taught you what you were supposed to hide about yourself? Which of these dark parts of you leak out—or explode—in private? And what impact has all of this had on your relationship with, and expression of, your authentic self? Do you even know who your authentic self is?

You see, you not only have had angels who helped you keep your authentic self alive as you grew up. You also had teachers who, often inadvertently, showed you how to develop your other two selves. A big part of stepping into your authenticity is to succeed at doing what Elvis didn't: ending your bondage to both your public self and the dark private self, which is in many cases your public self's opposite, so you can fully step into spiritually aligned authenticity.

In my conversations with Elvis, I didn't realize at the time that the groundwork was being laid for a point in my life where I would reconcile my three selves. That inner voice that I am asking you to listen to had spoken to me for over thirty-four years before I found the courage to answer and step into my true, authentic self.

How many times have you heard, "Listen to your heart"? Such a simple statement it is, but I want to encourage you to do just that. For it is truly that voice which introduces you to the gifts God has for you.

Questions to Ponder...

Each of your selves has had powerful teachers. Write down those teachers, identifying what you learned from each one about the authentic self, the dark private self, and the public self.

Now, think about the fundamental core beliefs that influenced you as you grew up. Write them down.

- Why DO you believe as you do?
- Is it because of rules, traditions, fear, and head knowledge? Or is it because of a deep inner experience?

In answering these questions you've taken another step toward living more fully from your authentic self.

CHAPTER THREE

THE AUTHENTIC KING

The authentic self that emerged when Elvis was out of the public eye was even more amazing than the icon his fans loved. Those of us who knew him well saw much more than the icon.

Although Elvis was among the most gifted of entertainers, his deepest gifts lived within the parts of his authentic self that he kept hidden from most of the world. For Elvis, this private authentic self was philosopher, mystic, and healer. And, for me, my most influential teacher.

Although he knew he was a talented entertainer, Elvis recognized that he had been blessed with these gifts. And for me as his apprentice, it was those gifts that would affect my life the most.

Not long after I arrived at Graceland, I began to witness the mystical sides of Elvis's authentic self.

I remember being around eight when I got a glimpse into this side of him for the first time. He, his then wife-to-be Priscilla, and I were laying by the pool at his home in Memphis. He always enjoyed getting some sun before shooting his next film or going out on tour.

"Elvis, we're not going to get any sun today," I said. "It's just way too cloudy." With that, Elvis lifted his right hand, and as he moved it, the clouds moved as well. Suddenly, the sun shone brightly. I looked on in total amazement. "Wow. That was cool." Often a man of few words, particularly when he did things like this, he silently nodded and winked.

Even though I couldn't wrap my mind around what I saw Elvis do, asking him how he did it somehow didn't feel necessary. He had such an overwhelming presence that when he did something extraordinary, I almost came to expect it.

The outside-the-box things I saw Elvis do continued to contradict what my mother's church was instilling in me about what mere mortals were capable of doing. But, I accepted them for what they were. During those formative years, I couldn't explain what I repeatedly saw, but they were also impossible for me to ignore.

Oftentimes during the steamy Memphis summers, we'd go outside and someone in the group would complain about the heat. One particularly sweltering day, a number of us were on the front steps of the Graceland mansion. One of the guys blurted out, "God, it's hot." Elvis lifted his hand, moved it from left to right, and a cool breeze blew across Graceland's front steps. I heard the sound of the blowing leaves in the trees as I felt refreshed by the wind on my face.

On another occasion, in 1967, a number of our friends and family gathered at Elvis's house in Los Angeles for a cookout. Suddenly, someone pointed up at the sky. We looked up just in time to see a mysterious object before it slipped behind some clouds. Once again, Elvis moved his hand; the clouds seemed to move in response, and suddenly we could again see the odd object.

For me, the UFO was merely a sideshow. The main event was his ability to move clouds at will. Later that night, Elvis and Priscilla, my brothers Billy and Ricky, my mother, and stepfather Vernon were sitting in the dining room when I looked at Elvis and said, "That was cool today." As always, he simply nodded and winked.

By the time I officially started working for him at sixteen, Elvis knew that his unusual gifts had become normal to me. Over the years, all I'd have to say to him was, "Elvis...." and he'd laugh as he'd move the clouds yet again.

Yes, we joked about it. But, this was very real. It was 1976. We were driving from Las Vegas to Elvis's home in Palm Springs—Elvis, myself, and his then-girlfriend Mindy Miller. At one point during the drive, we came upon a severe desert downpour, which was blowing from left to right in front of us. The sunroof was open. I'm thinking to myself, "Okay, Elvis, you've moved a few clouds and created several wind gusts, but this is a massive storm." I laughed out loud saying from the back seat, "Elvis, you've got to shut that sunroof unless you can do something about that storm!"

He threw me a quick sideways glance through the rear view mirror. Then, without hesitation, he lifted his arm through the sunroof, motioned his hand from left to right, and the storm parted. That's right. On the right side of the road it was pouring down rain. On the left side of the road it was pouring down rain. But the road on which we were travelling was now glistening; the sun's beaming light showing us the way home. Mindy was speechless.

Elvis's ability to move the clouds and make the wind blow was merely the tip of the iceberg. It's not only what he did but also how he carried himself while he was doing it. There's no question that he had magnetism and charisma, but it was more than that. Elvis had an aura around him that I always saw.

I first noticed it onstage when he made his comeback to live performance in 1969 in Las Vegas. When he walked out on stage that night at the then International Hotel (now the Hilton), I felt an energy that to this day continues to infuse my soul.

He'd not been on stage for nearly nine years, and this was his comeback to live performance. Behind his charisma, I felt an even more powerful presence. This was the Elvis the public loved. This was the Elvis who was the undisputed king. This was the Elvis who was the iconic public self. This

THE AUTHENTIC KING   45

Elvis was driven by the authenticity that came through his charisma, his magnetism, his music, and his showmanship.

His aura was ever-present onstage at every one of the hundreds of concerts I saw him perform when I was on tour with him during the seventies. Even in his later years, when he became overweight and slurred his words, his presence on stage, and its effect, was mesmerizing. It was this glow, this aura, this light around him that made Elvis different. People were drawn to him. Of course he could sing. But, there was more to him than that, because he could merely stand on stage and the crowd would go wild. Often without knowing why.

Looking back I now understand why; they were responding to his aura. To his gifts. To the public part of the authentic Elvis. Yes, he was sexy, yes he could sing, and yes the girls swooned. But, it was the authentic Elvis that made Elvis, Elvis.

"If my spiritual life isn't known, then my real story won't ever come out."
~ Elvis Presley

Elvis recognized his more-than-unusual gifts and always felt called upon by God to use them well. He had survived his twin brother's death at birth with the enduring question, "Why me?"

He always believed he survived for a reason. He felt he was obligated to God to discover whatever that was and to do it. I've often wondered how heavy a cross this was for him to bear.

This is why Elvis searched so intensively beyond the boundaries of the beliefs he was raised with.

There could be no doubt that the Bible was amongst his favorite books, and that it certainly laid the foundation for his fundamental core beliefs. But, ever since I could remember, there were always dozens of other books next to his bed. He was a seeker and he wanted answers.

Many of these books had been provided by someone Elvis referred to as "a messenger"; Larry Geller. He and Elvis had become friends during the filming of one of Elvis's pictures, *Roustabout*.

Larry, a prominent Hollywood hairdresser, had been called in to do Elvis's hair in 1964. There was an instant bond between the two of them. Larry was a passionate seeker himself. By the time they met, he had long been immersed in metaphysical philosophy. He was far different from all the others who worked for and surrounded Elvis. Larry quickly became the one person Elvis confided in, and trusted enough to open up to, about his spiritual quest and his unusual gifts.

This was important to Elvis because of how spiritually isolated he felt. He once said, "I know, some of the things that I think are kind of far out... and I don't meet a lot of people that I can relate to, and those that I do meet that need to know more about their spiritual selves, I do the best that I can, but I would like to be in a position to reach these people that are out there, I know that, and I can't get in that position. My career won't allow it, my management won't allow it, and many of my family and friends wouldn't understand it."

I met Larry when I was just a boy, soon after he started working for Elvis. Hip, mellow, eccentric, and West Coast, he couldn't have been any more different from my Southern roots. When I thought of "hippie" I thought of him. But it didn't take me long to discover that he was more than that.

Ironically, Larry was more like Elvis than anyone else in his inner circle. They were spiritual brothers, and Elvis came to look upon him as his principal spiritual advisor. In Larry's most recent book, *Leaves in Elvis's Garden,* he quotes Elvis as having confided to him that if even one person could be led to God because of iconic status, it would be worth any risks that might be involved.

For some in the inner circle, this didn't sit well. They thought Larry's influence on Elvis could be detrimental to his image. Elvis didn't agree. He wanted the public to know about his spiritual seeking, the books he was reading, and the mystical gifts he had. I too didn't see Larry as a threat. I always found him to be kind, gentle, and a dear friend, as he remains to this day.

The first book Larry gave Elvis later became the first book Elvis gave me. I believe the reason *The Impersonal Life* was so important to Elvis was that it opened the door to his accessing the God within, his true authentic self.

This book had a profound effect on Elvis. It changed his life.

Through this simple little book, he shifted out of believing that God's existence was only in Heaven, and into experiencing the God who lives within us all. "Be still and know that I am God," was a quote from the book, a phrase that rang out in his life from that day forward. It also awakened him to a broader vision of the search for knowledge no matter what its source. This is why he became perpetually surrounded by literally hundreds of metaphysical books containing other perspectives than those of the Bible.

The Impersonal Life gave him a better understanding of where his gifts came from and why God had given them to him. This enabled him to embrace that he was not only a gifted singer but a modern day mystic. This realization humbled him and helped him further anchor his personal belief that he had been handpicked for something greater than entertaining alone.

Just as Elvis discovered he had been handpicked, he handpicked me. He would often say to Larry, "We're getting David ready. He's got the gift." This was his intention in giving me *The Impersonal Life*. He knew a day would come when this simple book would open my heart and mind in ways that were similar to what it had done for him.

"Whatever I become will be what God has chosen for me."
~ Elvis Presley

Elvis went through a period of seriously contemplating leaving show business completely in order to lead more people to a spiritual path. Fortunately for his fans, I believe Elvis discovered that since his gifts as a musician and entertainer were God-given; God had wanted him to draw people to a spiritual life through those gifts. The fact is, his music was his message, the stage was his pulpit, and his audiences were his congregation.

Among many other things, *The Impersonal Life* led Elvis to the doorstep of Paramahansa Yogananda's Self-Realization Fellowship. SRF's first leader following Yogananda's death in 1952 was Sri Daya Mata. He arranged a number of private meetings with her.

Personally, I feel that he was drawn to SRF because Yogananda was the first high profile Eastern guru who explicitly connected Eastern teachings with the teachings of Christianity. Elvis knew what an influence he was on others and wanted to be sure that his explorations beyond the Bible would be in service to the glory of God.

I went with him to one of his final visits with Daya Ma, as she was fondly referred to, in the early 1970s. I remember walking with him through the SRF meditation gardens in Los Angeles, enchanted by the beauty and the sounds of nature in this urban oasis. Elvis was much like me: fidgety, impatient, always in motion. But, as we drew closer to Daya Ma's presence I noticed calmness come over him; as though a young apprentice was preparing to meet with his master.

We were ushered into a room where Elvis and Daya Ma were to meet. When she entered the room, Elvis approached her. They talked quietly between themselves as I waited on the other side of the room. As I witnessed their conversation from afar, I had a sudden sense of being in the midst of the divine. There was Elvis Presley and Sri Daya Mata, standing face-to-face illuminated in a brilliant bright light, as though the two were one.

After awhile, Elvis gestured toward me, saying, "David, this is Daya Mata." I came over and extended my hand to shake hers. Her hand was soft, her touch gentle, and her eyes soothing. I didn't know much about her at the time, but I did know that I was standing in the midst of greatness.

Elvis's spiritual explorations were far more than merely philosophical. He was also a healer who understood that the source of healing was through the Christ that lived within him. The laying-on-of-hands is common in the Pentecostal First Assembly of God, in which Elvis was brought up.

"How are you feeling, David?" Elvis would ask. When I would say, for instance, "Not so good today, I've got a headache." He would immediately say, "Sit down." He would place his hands on my head and simply pray, "Be still and know that I am God. God flow through us. In the name of Jesus, I pray that this pain leave David's body." It always did.

During the years I spent with Elvis I saw him do many remarkable spiritual healings from his authentic self. Yet, none touched my heart like the one that I witnessed him do during a concert in Boston in 1975.

Part of my responsibilities while on tour with Elvis was to make sure security was in place at the front of the concert stage before his performances. On this particular evening, I went out on the stage like I had done so many times before. Exiting the stage, I noticed a group of people in a reserved area that all of us on tour considered the "VIP" section. On this particular night, there was one young man in the section that caught my eye. He was in a wheelchair. His arms twisted in and his legs turned inward. In his hands he grasped a frame with the words to a song, "Impossible Dream." I knew this song because Elvis often included it in his set. As I drew closer I noticed at the bottom of the lyrics in broken handwriting he had written, "My impossible dream is to meet Elvis Presley."

This was one dream that I knew I could make come true. I walked up to the young man in the chair, placed a backstage pass on his shirt, and informed his parents he was coming with me.

I rolled him backstage to Elvis's dressing room and told a policeman to keep his eye on him, that I would be right back. I entered Elvis's dressing room where he was putting the finishing touches on his hair just moments before his concert.

"Elvis, there is someone I want you to meet."

"David, you know better than that. I don't see anyone before I go on stage."

"But Elvis, this is somebody special."

Reluctantly, Elvis said, "Okay, bring him in. This better be good."

I brought the boy into the dressing room. When he saw Elvis, his eyes lit up. His disease-riddled body began to shake. With every ounce of energy he could muster up, he slurred "ELVIS."

When Elvis saw him, he was so overcome with emotion he simply walked over, fell on his knees next to the boy, dropped his head in his lap and began to weep. Still grasping the frame the young man began stroking Elvis's hair with his crippled hand.

This was the most beautiful sight that I had ever witnessed. Elvis had met politicians, royalty, celebrities, and spiritual leaders but in spite of all that, he was most humbled by what he saw in this incredible young man.

After a moment I tapped Elvis on the shoulder, leaned down and whispered in his ear, "Boss, we've got to go. You got a show to do."

He stood up and regained his composure. "Make sure you take care of my friend here."

"Consider it done, Boss."

Instead of taking him back to his section, I kept him right next to me, assuring he had the best seat in the house. Elvis came out on stage that night to a massive crowd full of energy and excitement. He ripped through one song after another leaving the crowd begging for more.

Suddenly, Elvis turned to his music coordinator and whispered, "Impossible Dream."

At the sound of the first notes, the smile on the young man's face grew bigger. I had an assistant help me pick the boy's wheelchair up and place it on the corner of the stage. Elvis caught a glimpse of this and walked over and sang directly to him.

Tears rolled down the young man's face. His impossible dream was coming true, right before my very eyes. The boy held up the frame. It wasn't until that moment that Elvis saw the handwritten phrase, "My impossible dream is to meet Elvis Presley." He took the frame from the boy's hands as he sang the last lyric, "to reach the unreachable star."

In the hundreds of concerts that I had done with Elvis Presley, there had never been a time where the audience did not give a standing ovation after one of his songs. On this night, instead of applause, the only thing that could be heard was the sound of tears from 20,000 people dropping on the concrete floor of the sold out concert hall.

The love that Elvis showed that night toward that young man was as Christ like as anything I had ever seen in my life. In that moment, Elvis saw the perfection of this crippled man. What's more, this young man felt his own perfection and saw himself as Christ would see him. He experienced Elvis's gift of healing firsthand. As a result, his life would never be the same again. This was the authentic side of Elvis Presley that the public was drawn to.

Questions to Ponder...

- What have you read in your lifetime that opened your spiritual eyes in a way that is similar to the impact *The Impersonal Life* had on Elvis and me? Did you embrace the expanded vision of your authentic spiritual self that this book inspired, or did you pull back, afraid of what someone might think or say?

- Is your life leading you toward authenticity? If not, what barriers do you feel are keeping you from yourself?

- What miracles have you experienced in your life? Were you teachable enough to allow these to expand your vision of spirit, your authentic self, and your understanding of what's possible in life? Or did you shrink away from these, dismissing them as coincidences or one-of-a-kind oddities?

- Revisit the events you described above in light of what you read in this chapter. Ask yourself whether these were orchestrated by wisdom greater than you. If so, what gifts have you not yet discovered and harvested from these experiences? Are you ready to embrace these gifts now, even if others don't approve? When you have experiences like these in your life from now on, just try accepting them rather than explaining it through your preexisting beliefs.

CHAPTER FOUR

THE OTHER SIDE OF GREATNESS

The sheltered years of my informal childhood apprenticeship to Elvis had been filled with the magic of moving clouds and exposure to the vast light side of his private greatness.

This age of innocence ended for me in 1972, when Elvis asked me to go to work for him.

I was just sixteen when I climbed aboard his luxurious tour plane. Soon after, I was introduced to another Elvis: his dark side that privately accompanied the authentic self I had grown up around. Suddenly, I was being initiated into a whole new world of unaccountability and deceit. The contrast between life with Elvis inside Graceland and life with him on the road was staggering.

Elvis's professional life was one of extreme giftedness and talent. While his personal life lacked accountability, his public life was all about image. Here was this extraordinary charismatic talent who was privately on a spiritual quest, and yet also privately indulging his own inner demons. No one was allowed to draw those demons to his attention. Herein lies the lack of accountability that ultimately cost him his life.

In my five years working for him I learned a lifetime's worth about the dark private self we all have. This chapter is about that self. In Elvis, in me, and in you.

For me, Elvis's world now became compelling and confusing, attractive and repulsive, exciting and dangerous. It mixed impulsivity with discipline, loyalty with lies, and spirituality with ego. Indulging our dark selves privately was mostly fine... as long as it remained private. I was drawn to this excitement and devastated by the secrets that accompanied it.

I became intrigued and intoxicated by this new lifestyle. Diversions from my authentic self waited at every turn, although at sixteen I didn't care about authenticity. I didn't even know what it was.

But, what I did quickly learn was Elvis's version of loyalty. He often said, "You're either with me or against me." And, for me, there was no question that I was "with" him. Unconditionally.

A big part of being "with him" meant extremely high levels of secrecy. "Deny everything" was an unbreakable rule. What this meant was that we, his inner circle, were to never, ever, say anything to anyone about what went on in private that might conflict with Elvis's sanitized public iconic self.

Accountability meant guarding Elvis's public image. Loyalty meant hiding his improprieties and prescription drug abuse... and not confronting him about his private dark self.

Until I boarded his tour plane, I had no idea that Elvis took any medication, let alone how extensive his prescriptions' list was. Accompanying him wherever he went was a black kit containing a portable pharmacy of drugs that had been prescribed by a variety of doctors. I didn't think much about this at first, but over the years I came to clearly see that he was addicted to prescription medication, and that my responsibility was to watch over him as best I could.

The medications gradually engulfed Elvis in the self-destructive, downward spiral mindset of "give me more." During the last year of his life, a typical night would include over thirty sleeping pills and up to nine shots of Demerol over a twelve-hour span. These were countered during the day by an assortment of amphetamines and other stimulants, also prescribed by his doctors. Highly addictive medications took Elvis from a virile god to a broken man who needed to be closely monitored every minute of every day.

Little by little, Elvis's authentic self became increasingly eclipsed by his unwillingness to recognize or get help with his addiction. He didn't think he was addicted. The doctors gave him drugs and that was justification enough for him.

Whenever I raised my concerns about his escalating prescription drug abuse, his response was the same as any addict's: anger. "I'll decide what enough is." Translation: "You're with me only if you don't challenge my use of medication."

I knew at the time that his drug use was just a symptom of something deeper. Although I didn't yet know what that deeper thing was. The days of my life were those I spent helplessly watching the man I'd known and loved since my childhood gradually destroy himself.

As much as I loved him, I would look at him with total disdain as he lay in a hospital bed following one of his several accidental overdoses. He knew I was rattled, disappointed, and disgusted by what he was doing. Here was the greatest person I knew, someone with massive worldly and spiritual gifts, messing up royally.

There were three things Elvis loved in addition to his faith: his family, his fans, and his medications. If you messed with any of these things, chances are you'd be out on the street. The only ones in his inner circle who repeatedly confronted him on his prescription drug use were his closest friend from high school, Red West, and his cousin, Sonny West. Their confrontations would eventually get them fired in 1975. Personally, I believe that when Elvis fired them, he fired his conscience. From that day on, his drug use intensified and the end came quickly.

However, it didn't matter how large the inner conflict among his three selves grew prior to this untimely death. Whenever Elvis stepped onto the stage, he found a way to set this conflict aside just enough to somehow allow his authentic Presence to shine through. I believe this is why he continued to deeply move his audiences right through to his very last concert.

My intimately personal knowledge of the magnitude of his private gifts and private struggles leads me to conclude that this was not merely a miracle. It was a testament to the depth of his God-given gifts and his devotion to remaining His servant no matter what condition he might have been in.

Much has been said about who was to blame for Elvis Presley's untimely death. Some blame his management for over-working him. Many have blamed his doctors, who it often seemed to me were more concerned with their back pockets than his wellbeing. Still others have blamed me for not having watched him closely enough on the day he died.

But, in the end, it was Elvis who killed Elvis. It was his dark inner self, and his inability to face it, that destroyed him physically.

"I do not understand what I do. For what I want to do I do not do, but what I hate I do." ~ Romans 7:15

Indulging the dark side and ignoring the consequences has caused the greatest of men to sacrifice their authenticity, their values, their greatness, and ultimately their lives. It was this that I would spend the next three decades of my life trying to get out of my system, literally retraining myself to live in a very different way from my hero and role model.

There's no doubt in my mind that his escalating prescription drug addiction resulted in Elvis's death. But that's not what I believe really killed him. What causes icons, and the rest of us, to travel down such a self-destructive path? I believe the following toxic prescription cost Elvis his life, and threatens to do the same for anyone else who uses it:

- Protect your sanitized public image no matter what the cost to you or those you care about
- Deny or justify your dark private self no matter what the cost to you or those you care about
- Deny the extent to which protecting your public self and hiding your dark self impairs your authentic self
- Eliminate anyone who calls your attention to any of this
- Be taken down by your private darkness while publicly pretending it isn't happening

Elvis was, by far, not the first or the last that signed on to this toxic prescription. There's not a single public figure that doesn't struggle with it to one extent or another. And, the stronger your Presence and spiritual authenticity, the more intense this struggle tends to become. This is true of entertainers, athletes, politicians, and high-powered CEOs. However, no one, child or adult, public figure or everyday person, is exempt from the ravages that result when our three selves collide.

Michael Jackson slid down the same slippery slope that eventually cost him his life. Like Elvis, though arguably to a lesser extent, I believe Michael had a God-given magnetism and charisma, and was powerful and persuasive.

During an interview that my niece Lisa Marie Presley did with Oprah in 2011, she talked about her marriage, her life, and the death of her late husband. She openly revealed that no one said "no" to Michael, and she insinuated that if you did you wouldn't be around very long. She talked about his isolation, and how he felt he couldn't go anywhere or do anything in public. She came to recognize that no one could save Michael. As I watched her interview with tears in my eyes, I wanted to call Lisa to share with her how much I sympathized with and understood her, because I had lived through the exact same challenges with her father when she was just nine years old.

What also struck me was that Michael became Lisa's angel, of sorts, teaching her some of the same painfully priceless lessons about our three selves that I learned through Elvis.

What happens when our three selves collide? We *always* seek help. The question is, to whom or what do we look for that help?

When we don't seek help from other people or God, or we seek it but don't find the help we need, there is only one other form of help available to us. Anesthetics.

Anything in the world can be used as anesthesia when that's our intent. Not only alcohol, other drugs and food, but sex, power, adoration, accomplishments, possessions... not to mention watching TV, surfing the internet, playing computer games, reading, creative pursuits, sleep, and even psychological or spiritual development.

Anesthetics are hiding strategies that keep us from the pain of living out of integrity with our authentic self. The more we use anesthetics the more dependent on them we become. The price of escalating dependence is increasing destructiveness toward ourselves, others, and our work. That destructiveness either becomes intense enough to serve as a wake-up call or it becomes intense enough to maim and ultimately kill us, whether psychologically, spiritually, relationally, or physically.

As you now know, most people never knew what a mystical seeker and powerful healer Elvis was. Nor were they privy to the full extent of the damage created by the self-defeating behaviors that remained hidden from public view until years after his death. It was this gap between his dark private self and his authentic spiritual self that caused Elvis great misery. So much misery that when I asked, "Why the medications?" he always replied, "I'd rather be unconscious than miserable."

With this in mind, try to imagine the extent of his inner conflict. Imagine how limiting it was for Elvis to be someone whose iconic public self was not merely adored but worshipped by millions. His managers wanted to keep the extent of Elvis's spiritual seeking as private as possible in order to not risk threatening that image. Can you imagine how imprisoned Elvis might have felt by the expectations that his sanitized public self encouraged people to have of him?

Imagine the conflict Elvis had because he decided to keep hidden from view some of the most precious parts of his authentic spiritual self. Imagine the toll that keeping his dark self as private as possible took on him and those closest to him.

Now go beyond Elvis. To other public figures you've read about. To people in your own personal and work life, and perhaps to yourself as well. What do you think happens to our less-than-savory parts when we feel pressure to only show others our sanitized public self? Do you think that willpower alone can keep someone's dark self hidden forever, or make it magically disappear?

Though Elvis is physically dead he's far from gone. I believe that what continues to call to and inspire us even more than his music, movies, and legend, is his Presence, his true authentic spirit. However, if we ignore the struggles that led to his demise we deprive ourselves of one of the biggest gifts Elvis left for us: the importance of facing and resolving the gap between our own sanitized public self and our dark private self.

It would take me decades following his death before I at last discovered this gift. And it is through this that I became able to begin to fully embrace my authentic spiritual self.

Questions to Ponder...

Before you move to pondering this chapter's questions below, I want to first review the lessons we've covered so far in the book:

1. **All of us have three selves: our public sanitized self, our private dark self, and our authentic and often largely private spiritual self.** Chapter One gave you glimpses into Elvis's three selves and invited you to identify yours.

2. **We in large part develop all three of these selves in response to what we learn from others, whether through observation, words, or both.** Chapter Two showed you some of the ways I built my three selves primarily on Elvis's shoulders, and to a lesser extent on the shoulders of my mother and her denomination. You then had an opportunity to reflect on who you modeled your three selves after.

3. **Only one of our three selves is fully authentic, although most of us express aspects of our authentic self through our public sanitized**

self. There is a very important reason that Elvis's iconic public self was as powerful, charismatic, and magnetic as it was. That reason was the magnificence of his authentic self. In Chapter Three, you read examples of the profound and unusual gifts I and others were blessed with by Elvis's more private aspects of his authentic self. You also got a couple of glimpses into the devotion he had to finding ways of sharing these gifts with the public despite the significant limitations his iconic public self placed on him. At the end, you got to explore the differences among your three selves.

4. **Our three selves are in conflict:** The more sanitized our public self becomes, the more private the dark parts of us become. Even though we try to keep these dark parts private, they neither disappear nor stop influencing us. Quite the contrary. The more private we keep them the larger they grow, even if outside our awareness. And the larger they grow the more they eclipse the brilliance of our authentic spiritual self. Just as happened with Elvis, and with me.

Keeping these first four lessons in mind I now invite you to ponder these questions....

- What anesthetics do you use?
- Where in your life do you feel entitled? What do you believe you should be allowed to get away with?

- What ugliness did you learn was acceptable to express toward others?
- What are your strongest self-defeating patterns?
- What prices have your dark side cost you? And others?
- How have you tried to downplay or minimize those costs?
- What aspects of your authenticity become hard for you or others to access in moments when your dark side is running the show?
- Where would your dark side ultimately take you if you ignored and indulged it for long enough?

CHAPTER FIVE

TRYING EVERYTHING BUT GOD

Although Elvis had left many impressions on my life, the ones I initially emulated most were the dark sides of Elvis's greatness. I, too, used anesthetics that were detrimental to both my personal and professional lives. Soon after I went to work for Elvis and saw the darker side of reality, I found myself longing for the values my mother had instilled in me as a young man.

It was while on the road that I was introduced to the world of sex, drugs, and rock-and-roll, and the accompanying I-me-mine mentality of "if it feels good do it." Oftentimes feeling guilty, I didn't know what to do about this inner conflict. I tried to get away from this by quitting for a short time. But, my loyalty to Elvis was too strong for that to work.

My authentic self went against what I saw and lived on the road with Elvis. Not knowing how to navigate this conflict set me up to make some very serious mistakes that not only hurt me, but many innocent ones around me.

I couldn't explain at the time what didn't feel right about working for Elvis. So, in 1974, at seventeen, I made a second attempt at getting away from my darkness by getting married. Angie was a fine, upstanding, Christian girl. She was everything good that I had been raised on, but stepped out of, when I started working for Elvis.

Even being married couldn't keep me from returning to work for Elvis. No one said "No" to him, least of all me. So, when he once again called to say he needed me, I was gone. Then, three years later, so was my short-lived marriage to Angie. My affairs, black book, drugs, and lack of accountability, were more than this young woman could handle.

Angie made the announcement that she was leaving me just two weeks before Elvis died. She had become my only connection with goodness, and now that goodness was leaving. To say I was crushed is an understatement.

Elvis tried to intercede by calling us into his room and praying with us. He felt that he could talk her out of leaving. But, Angie was no fool, nor was I. She had every reason to leave, and in spite of all the miracles I'd seen Elvis do, this was one that he was unable to pull off.

When she left, she inadvertently took the ankh Elvis had given me at his home in Los Angeles in 1972 as part of my initiation into apprenticeship.

"David, I've taught you everything you know, but I haven't taught you everything that I know." ~ Elvis Presley

I had seen and learned a lot from Elvis over my years growing up with him; signs and wonders that I had been unable to comprehend. Unbeknownst to me, Elvis apparently thought that I had now seen enough to enter into an official apprenticeship. He sat me down, looked at me, and said, "David, there's no question that you have a teachable spirit. The time has come to broaden your horizons."

Soon after, he began giving me books on spirituality and mysticism, starting with *The Impersonal Life,* followed by *The Prophet, Living the Infinite Way,* and many others. He would ask me to read from these books, and this would be followed by discussion and meditation.

Elvis would put on a long, gold-laced, emerald green robe. He would have me sit on the bed with him in a meditation posture. He would always start our sessions by saying:

"David, close your eyes. Be still and know that I am God. Take three deep breaths. Still your body and mind, and breathe normally. Breathe through Christ's light, Christ's peace. Repeat this over and over.

"Surround with pure white light. Visualize yourself as strongly as possible and surround yourself with this Christ light. Keep yourself in tune with Christ of God within, completely trusting in Him. Completely."

After our meditations, we would talk about the subconscious and super subconscious minds, as well as the third eye. We talked about how all things were possible and the importance of meditation and breathing in expanding consciousness.

Frankly, half the things he said to me during these sessions I didn't understand. However, this connection I had with Elvis demonstrated to me how much he loved me and how important it was to him that I mature spiritually.

He would always say, "David, you have the gift of discernment. You have a high energy and a bright blue aura. You will do great things one day. And I will always be with you."

He extended my apprenticeship further by enrolling me in martial arts training. Not only to prepare me for becoming one of his bodyguards, but even more importantly to help me learn how to channel my energy and discipline my spirit. He viewed the martial arts as an outer expression of strength that was attained through inwardly harnessing control.

While I found this world with Elvis fascinating and intriguing, and experienced much spiritual growth from it, this also magnified my battle between my own dark side and authentic spiritual self.

In the end, Elvis's dark side would win. And all I was left with were his words to me in my last conversation with him two days before he died: "I'll always be with you. The next time I see you I will be in a different place on a higher plane."

Elvis's earthly struggles were over, but the war between my dark side and my authentic spiritual side continued to rage in me. I was lost. I now had no one to look to for guidance. I felt completely abandoned. Elvis was the only one I trusted. I couldn't trust the love of others because I didn't know whether they loved me because I was David or because I was related to a superstar.

With my still-undeveloped connection with my authentic spiritual self, I followed the darker side of his footsteps by turning even more strongly to anesthetics. My drug and alcohol intake that began during my years on tour with him now intensified. With no answers, I adopted the one philosophy I remembered the most: I'd rather be unconscious than miserable.

So desperate was I to communicate with Elvis in this place he called a higher plane and a different place, that I found myself in a séance in New York in 1978, while I was there writing my first book, *Elvis, We Love You Tender*. The medium and I sat in the room. Elvis's spirit was summoned. I indeed felt his presence. Except, rather than feeling relief I felt anger. For, at that time, I didn't want to feel anything. I simply wanted to see him. The séance didn't relieve my suffering.

When I returned to Memphis afterward, I was so deeply depressed that I took seventy-five Valiums along with a fifth of scotch. Was this me consciously trying to take my own life? No. But, if I did die I knew I'd see him.

My mother had gone out for the evening. When she came back home she saw me lying unconscious on the floor. Even at 5'2" and 125 pounds she somehow managed to drag my 6'3" 245 pound frame to the car and took me to the hospital. I woke up and there Elvis was, sitting on the bed with me. He said, "David, this is not the way. It's not your time. God's not done with you." As I listened, his voice was replaced by that of my mother's, who was on her knees praying, "God, please save my son. I know You have a plan for him."

When Elvis gave me the ankh back in 1972 he had told me the same thing I now heard in my mother's prayers: that God had a plan for me. I believe he came to my deathbed that day to remind me that this had not changed. Lying there with IVs in my arms and tubes in my nose, the doctor entered the room, looked directly at me, and said, "Young man, you're supposed to be dead."

From that day forward, I knew in my heart that God did indeed have a plan for me. Yet, this was confusing to me. Like Elvis, reconciling my authentic spiritual calling with the darkness that accompanied it became the challenge that sculpted my life from that day forward.

After I got home from the hospital, one of the first things I did was re-read my copy of *The Impersonal Life* that Elvis had given to me when I began my apprenticeship with him. "Be still and know that I am God." I just could not conceive of this.

Torn between the God of my mother and the broader vision of spirit that Elvis had exposed me to, I began to call out to God to reveal what was next for me. One night, lying in my bed, I heard a sound I didn't recognize. It was coming from a room down the hall that no one was in.

It was a Presence. I didn't know if it was God, Elvis, or the devil. I said, "Whoever you are, reveal yourself to me now." With that, a blackness rushed down the hall and entered me. Uncontrollably, I felt myself reaching for the gun I'd always kept next to my bed.

Unwillingly, my hand began to move it toward my head, pulling the hammer back during the process. Outside I could hear the sound of my dog howling over the Presence of whatever this was.

The gun continued to move toward my temple. I couldn't talk. I could barely breathe. Just as the gun got to my head with my finger firmly on the trigger, I somehow managed to yell out, "In Jesus' name, God help me." With those words, my body fell limp. The darkness was gone. The sound of the dog had stopped. I laid in a pool of cold sweat.

Suddenly, one of my roommates came out of her room and to my door, and said, "David, are you okay?" I was very much frightened and said, "What the hell was that?!" She said, "I don't know. All I could hear was moaning and growling that sounded like a demon wailing in despair from the depths of hell." We both were visibly shaken by this. But, I told her I was okay, even though I wasn't, and she returned to her room.

I somehow managed to fall asleep a little later, but was soon awakened. Elvis was sitting on my bed. "David," he said, "it wasn't me. It was the darkness. It's trying to kill you." He continued, "Be still and know that I am God. Be still, and know that I'll always be with you." And with that, he was once again gone.

What did this mean? Why was this happening to me? This wasn't the first nor the last time that Elvis came to me in such a way. Each time he did, he'd always remind me to "Be still and know that I am God. God is with you. I am with you."

I had nearly overdosed and later almost shot myself in the head. My life had now been spared twice. There had to be a reason, and I was determined to find it.

I had tried sex, drugs, and rock-and-roll. I had served the King of Rock and Roll. Now I felt it was time to serve the King of Kings. I was completely unprepared for any career other than as Elvis's bodyguard. Yet, I left Memphis with my new-found revelation, moved to Dallas, Texas, and entered the world of organized evangelism.

Questions to Ponder...

We all have had mentors, and most of them have been "mixed bags." Some of us have benefitted from having had a formal mentoring relationship with someone. For others of us, we have had long-term spiritually intimate relationships that have provided us with mentoring. And yet others of us have had mentors who never even knew they were our mentor. This might have been people we learned from by observing. Perhaps at work or school, in our community, our volunteer work, or our personal life. Or maybe characters from television, movies, or books have served as mentors to us.

Regardless of where we find our mentors, most of us gain priceless gifts from them. We often learn some unhelpful things from them as well. And sometimes we become fiercely loyal to them, for better and for worse.

Elvis was my first true mentor. He was the first person to initiate me into the world of spirituality. He was also the person who most influenced how I came to deal with the conflict we all have among our three selves.

Now it's your turn:

- Who was your first, or most important, mentor?
- What blessings did you receive from that mentoring?
- What did you learn from this mentor that later proved *unhelpful*?
- What types and amounts of loyalty did this mentor require of you?
- What was the biggest thing you didn't feel permission to challenge in this mentor?
- Did being loyal to this mentor require you to sacrifice some of your authentic self? If so, describe the sacrifices you made, and the prices that you and others you care about have paid because of the dysfunctional parts of your loyalty contract with this mentor.

- Who or what else have you been loyal to at the expense of your authentic self? What prices have you and others you've cared about paid because of this?
- Do you see why it is difficult to be loyal to mentors, or other people, who require you to sacrifice your authentic self?

CHAPTER SIX

FROM THE KING OF ROCK & ROLL

TO THE KING OF KINGS

All I had when I arrived in Dallas was my car, my mother's faith, and a desire to change my life. I now had a new job as the Director of Communications for a nationally prominent evangelist named James Robison. When I entered his office for my first meeting with him, I felt like I had walked into the executive suite of Apple's CEO. This was multi-million dollar evangelism. Up to this point in my life I hadn't known this type of ministry even existed.

A hunter and avid golfer, James's massively sized office was filled with deer heads, mounted fish, and photos of him with famous golfers and politicians. On his desk was a model of his private plane. Through the window was a twin building, which housed his television studio, magazine publishing operation, and of course a telephone call center that was receiving massive, ongoing tax-deductible donations.

Having been raised in a world in which preachers didn't make much money, this was unfathomable to me. I had walked into the world of Christian production at its highest level.

My new post was Director of Communications. My responsibilities included sound direction for not only James Robison's crusades, but for the speakers and musicians who went out each weekend to represent the ministry in towns and cities around the country. Each week staff singer John McKay, his pianist, and I would fly in one of the ministry's private planes to give a concert at churches throughout the country.

One Sunday, about three months after I began working, John asked me to share with the congregation my personal story about how I had gone from the King of Rock and Roll to the King of Kings. Needless to say, I was freaked out the first time I entered the pulpit. With my knees knocking and my voice quivering, I managed to share a twenty-minute story about how this ministry had reached into my home, touched my heart, and changed my life.

Before long, I got very good at giving my personal testimony before large groups. Life was good again. I was making a living, I had a nice apartment, and although the planes weren't as big as I was accustomed to in Elvis's fleet, I did enjoy the private planes and the lifestyle that accompanied them.

It didn't take long for word to get back to James Robison that I was an asset to the ministry and its donations. During one of his Crusades, in Huntsville, Alabama, ironically at the same coliseum I had been at with Elvis in 1976, James asked me to share my personal testimony. I boldly entered the platform and spoke about how this powerful ministry, and James Robison's message, had touched my life.

As I ended, 15,000 people stood to their feet and applauded as I left the stage. I walked past James and his other speakers and singers. They shook my hand, hugged me, and congratulated me on having told such a powerful story. I could hardly believe that I had just spoken from the same stage that Elvis had performed on three years before. That was the moment when this shy kid and former bad-ass bodyguard recognized his own gift of communication. This was a turning point in my spiritual journey. In the years to come, this gift would serve me well.

No sooner had I left the stage had James immediately walked onto the platform to take the customary love offering, saying, "We've reached through the gates of Graceland and touched the heart of Elvis's brother. Now, with your support, perhaps we can reach Elvis's former wife, Priscilla, and his daughter, Lisa Marie, as well."

It took a full twenty minutes for James's staff to pass the customary Kentucky Fried Chicken buckets all the way through the audience to receive their love offering.

After the offering was taken, I left the stage to take a nostalgic tour of the dressing room where I had been with Elvis previously when he performed. Finding it, I opened the door, and to my surprise there was the staff emptying tens of thousands of dollars out on the floor, carefully separating the checks from the cash.

I thought, "Wow, that's a lot of money. What a business this evangelism thing is."

I continued with James for another eight months, during which it became clear to me that I was his most prized trophy. Each night I spoke, the offerings were always the biggest.

I left James Robison to begin my own ministry. By then I had married my second wife, Kandis, for essentially the same reasons I had married my first wife, Angie. Like Angie, Kandis was pure, wholesome, sweet, and had a genuine relationship with Christ. I gravitated toward her out of the fear of God and hell that I had internalized from my mother's denomination.

I believed that Kandis would save me from myself. Outside of the occasional beer or two I was a good Christian husband. I got testimonials about my speaking abilities from the country's leading evangelists. Before long, I was spending forty-eight weekends of the year sharing my powerful testimony called "From the King of Rock and Roll to the King of Kings."

What many would consider a glamorous job was anything but. During the week I attended college. Every Friday I would drive to a nearby town in Texas and surrounding states to speak. Because I was only twenty-six, I spoke mostly at youth conferences and church youth services. However, because I was related to Elvis Presley, many adults also attended. The church ordinarily provided room and board. Mostly, this meant a hotel room where the roaches were oftentimes as big as me.

A love offering would be taken after I spoke, and this would be my pay. Many nights I would step into the pastor's office as they counted the offerings that had come in. Sometimes the pastor or deacons would pocket the bulk of the offering and give me a minimal amount of what had actually come in, telling me that this was all they received.

As disturbing as this was, it couldn't match when the wife of a pastor, deacon, or church member would show up at my motel door in much the same way that the women did while I was touring with Elvis. I never succumbed to this, but its effects had a devastating impact on me because these experiences stood in stark contrast to what I had been taught and at that time believed.

I had thought that by entering the field of evangelism I was leaving my rock and roll lifestyle behind. I must admit that I was pretty shocked to find out how wrong my assumption had been.

My ministry steadily grew and expanded to include the entire United States and later became international. In time, I found myself being courted by the top evangelists of the 1980s. They, like James, understood the value of me being a guest speaker during one of their crusades. The offering was always the biggest the night I spoke. I became disillusioned and realized that many of these individuals were using me. Even back then, my gift of discernment served me well. For, you see, before many of these evangelists took the fall, I could see the handwriting on the wall. Tammy Faye and Jim Bakker, Jimmy Swaggart, and local Texas evangelist Pastor Bob Tilton were all destroyed by the contradictions between their public image and what they did behind closed doors.

My will to live what was considered the Christian life also began to decay. This wasn't me. I had married Kandis, and entered the ministry, for all the wrong reasons. I felt their strengths would give me strength to overcome the negative ideologies of my rock and roll past.

The condemnation and judgmentalism that spewed out of my mouth from the pulpits of America and beyond contradicted the lessons of compassion and tolerance I had learned as Elvis's apprentice.

What disturbed me the most in my life as an evangelist was my discouragement of what I saw and experienced.

Much like Elvis, I became a public facade. "The image is one thing. The man is very much different." This reality worsened when I fell in love with a singer who regularly traveled with me. No stranger to infidelity, I lost all sense of reality, once again betraying the vows I had made to my wife.

All this time, while I was living a lie, thousands continued to be enlightened by God's word. Obviously, there was still something very much missing from my life. If the pastors, their staffs, and congregations knew the secret life I was again living, would they condemn me to hell?

I could not stop thinking about, nor ignore, the miracles that I'd seen in Elvis's life during my seventeen years with him. But, he too was far from perfect, and God still used him in mighty ways. I remember speaking one night when an evangelist stood up next to me and proclaimed that Elvis was in hell. Needless to say, this angered me. Here was a group of people who proclaimed the forgiveness of God but so quickly judged the blacks, the gays, and the rock and rollers of our world.

It finally hit me; this was not right.

When I entered evangelism, my heart was in the right place, but now my private actions no longer matched the public message I was preaching. Despite enjoying growth and success in this world, I ultimately came to the conclusion that I myself had become nothing more than yet another predator in the pulpit.

I couldn't live with my hypocrisy any longer. I went to Kandis and told her the truth, which understandably cost me my marriage. I then told the truth to my singer's husband. My next stop was my pastor. Here was a good man that put his entire reputation on the line by endorsing my ministry, and I had let him down.

My next meeting as an evangelist would be my last. As I entered the pulpit that night, I looked out at the thousands in the congregation and openly confessed the contradiction between my values and my transgressions. While sharing this, I could feel anger and disappointment welling up in the souls of many. But, I stood firm like a lion and, with a newly emerging feeling of personal power that only comes from becoming authentic, reminded this congregation what the Bible clearly teaches: He who is without sin, let him cast the first stone.

While too many churches are filled with professional stone-throwers, none were flung that night. For, you see, just prior to leaving the pulpit, I asked those who were willing to be honest with themselves and God to meet me at the altar to seek His mercy. Hundreds flooded the altar to get right with God. In the thirteen years I had spent in evangelism, my last message from the pulpit was perhaps the most powerful one I had yet communicated. Needless to say, a lot of healing took place that night.

Looking back on this part of my spiritual journey, I am reminded of a song performed by Christian artist Russ Taff back in the late '80s and written by Michael Been and James Goodwin.

The central theme in the lyrics of "I Still Believe" has an eternal place in my heart despite all the trial and tribulations that I experienced during this part of my spiritual journey.

While I am not proud of those years, and consider them perhaps the darkest chapters of my life, I did learn more about faith and forgiveness than

I ever had before. When I left that night, I left the world of ministry and organized religion, for good.

"I Still Believe."

My evangelism years were the portion of my spiritual journey in which I tested my mother's faith. I immersed myself in it with heart and soul. What I discovered at the other end was that the evangelistic mindset didn't fit for me anywhere near as well as the authentic spiritual faith that Elvis had exposed me to. I believe that one of the most important reasons so many people were touched by and continue to love Elvis was because his faith was pure, unconditionally nonjudgmental, and embracing of all faiths and people.

This, to me, is an expression of the heart of the teachings of Jesus. Judgmentalism and condemnation have done huge damage in the name of religion. Not only has it shut out the greatness of God's light, it has confined many minds and the hearts of millions around the world who believe that in order to have a relationship with God they need to be controlled by dos and don'ts rather than healed by the grace and mercy of God's unconditional love.

In the end, judgmentalism and condemnation have no place in this world. It's this over-controlling mindset that actually creates our dark private self. We hide what we learn that people fear and hate in us, and in themselves.

Except, whatever we push into darkness within us never dies. It merely goes underground and expresses itself indirectly or behind closed doors, while we continue to show the world our sanitized public self in the hope that people will never see what we've hidden within.

This is what I believe trapped and ultimately destroyed Elvis physically. This is where I became trapped during my evangelism years, and this may be where you are today as well. If so, please understand that this is a prescription for spiritual, psychological, and physical self-destruction, not for spiritual authenticity and enlightenment.

I believe that God loves, nurtures, and receives all people from all walks of life, from all faiths and denominations.

I believe that God gives life and love, and provides a bright beacon of light in a world of darkness.

I believe you have a teachable spirit or you wouldn't be reading this book.

No matter where you are in your life or your spiritual journey, I encourage you to take a moment right now, before you go on, to find within you the courage to allow your transgressions to be illuminated by the light of God. Once you have done this, embrace the greatness of what God means you to be, and take your next step forward in embodying your true authentic self.

Questions to Ponder...

Our authentic self is never self-destructive. Self-destructiveness comes from the tension between our sanitized public self and our private dark self. In other words, self-destructiveness is really "false self" destructiveness.

We all have, at times, made choices that proved to be harmful to ourselves or others. As well-intended people, when we discover we've done this, we do our best to clean up the mess and we also resolve to do something different in our future.

How do we do this? Society teaches that the way to succeed is through a combination of good intentions and willpower. Yet, even the best of us end up repeating some of our mistakes anyway, despite our good intentions and persistence. We then are baffled about how this repetition could have happened. Dr. Gruder's profound quote captures the answer: "We live our lives at the level of our wounds, not our wishes." My story in this chapter illustrates the first step in breaking free of being controlled by our baggage: coming clean about the damage we've done. We do damage despite our good intentions because the energy it takes to manage the split between our sanitized public self and our private dark self prevents the light of our authentic self from shining as brightly and ongoing as it is meant to.

This was the case for Elvis. Even though many of his fans have overlooked, through their adoration of him, the demons he unsuccessfully battled, that doesn't mean he didn't succumb to them. I followed in his footsteps, falling into the same oh-so-human traps during my evangelism years that I did during my Elvis years.

History is full of examples of people who have thrown stones at others for making mistakes instead of learning from their own. Elvis and I have both been on the receiving end of this. I'm confident that you have had similar experiences yourself. In the name of compassion, I encourage you to recognize this temptation as nothing more than a human attempt to deny the damage that we ourselves have done through our own versions of other people's mistakes.

Mistakes are never a problem. Not learning from them is.

Not taking responsibility for our human imperfections prevents us from becoming authentic. Now is your chance to come clean with yourself about your versions of what I did. Doing this is your next step in moving toward embodying your authentic self.

Select a big mistake you have made in your life that you vowed to not repeat, only to repeat it anyway, even if in perhaps a different form. Describe the following about this mistake:

- What was this particular big mistake that you ended up repeating despite your good intentions?

- How did you word the commitment you made to yourself about not repeating it in the future?

- What changes did you make in your inner attitudes or outer life in an attempt to not make that mistake again?

- What choices did you make that contributed to repeating this mistake anyway? (Don't focus on the outer circumstances that issued you the invitation to repeat this mistake, but instead on the inner choices you made in response to those circumstances.)

- What damage did you do to yourself and/or others because of the choice you made, even though you again did this damage despite your good intentions?

- What steps did you take to repair that damage? If you didn't take such steps, who did you at least share your transgressions with?

- What steps will you (or did you) take to free yourself from the baggage that caused you to repeat this mistake?

- What support will you get in taking these steps? (Because, as you'll see in the next chapter, isolation is the enemy of authenticity.)

ELVIS & DAVID ~ 1972

ELVIS & DAVID ~ 1976

CHAPTER SEVEN

ISOLATION: THE ENEMY OF AUTHENTICITY

My first taste of isolation came when my mother placed my two brothers and me in a boarding home in Virginia. She and Vernon put us there so it would be easier for her to make arrangements to marry Vernon.

When we arrived it was all bright smiles. My mother had no idea that as soon as they left, the smiles instantly turned to indifference. This was an old, dark, dirty, and dingy place. I remember having an ongoing feeling of abandonment. The staff was a group of older women who were strong on discipline and short on nurturing. Any outward show of emotion generally earned a dose of Tabasco sauce on our tongue as an act of discipline. There was no adult there who I felt safe with; no one to nurture me through this time in my life.

All that my two brothers and I had were each other. I would cry myself to sleep at night because I didn't understand where my parents were. My brother, Ricky, would come over to my crib and try to soothe me by saying, "David, don't cry. You'll see. Someday, things will get better."

When we moved into Graceland in 1960, things did indeed get better. When I found a new big brother in Elvis, my feelings of isolation faded. Or, rather, they took a hiatus. They returned when I started going to school.

As a speaker, I often incorporate in the early part of my talks how much attention I got from being dropped off at school in a pink Cadillac. The audience has always found it somewhat humorous as I remind them that this was before Mary Kay. The fact is that it did have a profound effect on my life.

I would get out of the car and walk toward the school, and it wouldn't take long for the ridicule to begin. "Hey, hound dog?" "What's up sideburns?" And of course the joke, "My brother lives under the steps." "Why's that," I'd ask. "Because he's my stepbrother."

Again, I hadn't asked to move into Graceland or be Elvis's brother. My brother Ricky has often said that being a stepbrother to Elvis Presley is a lot like being a Kennedy; it is both a blessing and a curse. For me as a child, the curse was the bullying I experienced at school because I was related to Elvis.

The jokes and ridicule were hard enough, but when the kids in school wanted to beat me up just because I was Elvis's brother, that's when I found myself withdrawing and keeping to myself. The only safe ground that I really had was on the grounds of Graceland. There I had my family, and the one person who understood this ridicule better than all of us: Elvis.

When I would talk to Elvis about my problems at school, he always tried to instill something positive in me. He would tell me that I was special, and that people were jealous of the life I had acquired at Graceland. He would then remind me about what it had been like for him when he was a kid in school, wearing flashy clothes, having sideburns, and being in the glee club rather than on the football team. He told me he couldn't count the times he had been on the receiving end of a brutal fist or verbal humiliation.

Gladys, his mother, had trusted no one. Vernon, my stepfather, didn't either. They believed that everyone had a hidden motive. And who could blame them? They had stepped from the poor cotton fields of rural Tupelo, Mississippi, into the spotlight of urban Memphis, Tennessee. And once Elvis became famous, everyone wanted a piece of him.

His mother was his most trusted ally, and in my opinion his biggest loss. I believe she was the only person he really ever trusted. Many of those who knew her told me that his success brought on so much worry in her that it became more than she could bear.

As a newcomer to this family, Vernon made it very clear that we never discussed Elvis's personal or professional life to anyone, anywhere, at any time. He also expected us to be extremely skeptical of everyone we met, and their intentions. This was very difficult for me as a child. It put me in a position where I believed I could never be close to anyone outside the family.

Of necessity, everything revolved around Elvis. While this is one reason why I became so close to him, the price of this intimacy was being isolated from the rest of the world. Our family's security needs eliminated much of the social life that I would have enjoyed as a child living somewhere other than at Graceland.

Because of this, in some very real ways, I didn't have a childhood. Starting to work for Elvis when I was only sixteen added to this dilemma because I never got to be a teenager either.

This was a life where friends and associates were handpicked. Everyone in Elvis's inner circle was either a family member or someone he had met very early in his life. These became the yes men; the ones who could never say no to Elvis. Unfortunately, as I grew older, I, too, would become one of them.

Because the only voice that mattered was Elvis's, I had no identity. Except in relation to Elvis. This disconnection from myself was the ultimate in isolation. It wasn't until I found my gift as a speaker that I finally began to develop my own sense of self.

When Elvis died, the one thing I had that most of the rest of his inner circle didn't was my youth. At just twenty-one years old I had the rest of my life to step out of the shadow of the King and define myself. In hindsight, I understand that this feeling of being nothing without him was a big part of what caused me to completely fall apart after he died, in addition to how deeply I loved him.

It was so bad for me that the first three years after his death I spent stoned, aimless, and unconscious. I managed to find jobs that kept a little food on the table, but other than that, life was as completely opposite from Graceland as you could get. This was how empty my life had become before I was offered a job with James Robison.

It didn't take me long to discover that in my attempt to move from the King of Rock and Roll to the King of Kings, I had traded one form of isolation for another. We as individuals are always looking for someone to trust. In my world of rock and roll, this was a trait rarely found or even expected. In my new world of evangelism, I believed this would be the one place where I would find trust.

After my departure from evangelism, I continued to speak throughout the 1990s. All that had changed was my congregation. In the corporate world I felt safe. Unlike many in the world of Christianity, this was a group of people who didn't bury their wounded.

By the time I started speaking in the corporate world, I had overcome my addictions of the past, completed my GED, gone to college, and begun to master my craft as a public speaker.

In my keynotes, I continued to use my story to inspire, motivate, and challenge people to turn their adversities into personal triumphs. I continued to do this by sharing the pitfalls of my life in rock and roll. I did this by focusing more on how isolation had destroyed Elvis rather than on his extraordinary gifts and the spiritual lessons I learned from him.

In the early 1990s, my focus on the circumstances of Elvis's death created much controversy. In an article I wrote with prolific author Albert Goldman, I openly talked about how Elvis's last comments to me, combined with his familiarity with drugs, led me to conclude that he had perhaps taken his own life.

What I later realized was that what I said in this article also did a lot of damage to the iconic image of Elvis. It upset many fans around the world who read it and this added to my isolation. What they didn't understand is that there is no fan out there who loved Elvis Presley as I did. No one felt more pain than I did when I walked into his bathroom to find his lifeless body. He was no king to me; he was my brother. He was such a profound teacher, not only about how to live but also about how not to live, that to ignore his dark side is to deprive ourselves from some of his most valuable lessons.

I think it is important for all to understand that while Elvis was perhaps one of the most influential men of the twentieth century, and a highly spiritually evolved individual who still touches millions of lives around the world, he was still just a human being with frailties and imperfections, just like you and me.

In the article, I made reference to how Elvis had said to me on many occasions during the last few years of his life that he "would rather be unconscious than miserable." Personal development guru Anthony Robbins picked up on this and quoted me in his classic book, *Awaken the Giant Within*. In it, he effectively illustrated the lesson I was trying to communicate about what drove Elvis to make such a comment.

I have done a lot of soul searching since that 1990 *Life Magazine* cover story appeared. My motivation for doing this article was to use my life with Elvis, and the tragedies that surrounded it, to help, motivate, and inspire others to not make the same mistakes that took his life.

It was never my intention to upset fans with this information. Since that time the world's grown up, and I continue to believe that if this revelation saved even one person from taking their own life, it was worth it.

It was important to me that the world look at the man I intimately knew who seemingly had everything and to understand that despite all he had, he ended up with nothing because of having driven himself into a state of terminal isolation.

This is the danger of isolation in its most dramatic form. In my world of evangelism I was saying one thing while doing another. For, you see, I had taken this unhealthy part of Elvis into that world. Fortunately, I gradually came to recognize yet another lesson that Elvis had left me with. It was about how unaddressed isolation can create toxic damage, as it had done in me.

Instead of allowing myself to be crushed by isolation, the way he did, I embraced transparency. I needed to do this because, like Elvis, the split between my public self and my dark private self was destroying me. I am profoundly grateful to him for modeling to me the dangers of isolation. The lessons we can learn from his tragic demise are just as powerful as those we can learn from his spiritual life. To ignore these lessons is to only learn from part of who Elvis really was, and this selective remembering only serves to diminish what Elvis's extraordinary life can teach us all.

Prior to Elvis's death no one knew the devastating condition that he was truly in toward the end of his life. Yes, there were signs of his deterioration. Weight gain. Slurring words on stage. Cancelled shows. But, the world had no idea what the price of isolation was costing the king.

Unfortunately for Elvis, his public image was about to be challenged. A tell-all book was about to be released exposing the huge dichotomy between the private Elvis and his public image. Two of the three authors of that book had for decades been at the very center of his life and career.

Elvis, myself, and others who worked for him saw the book galleys prior to its release. Needless to say, he was utterly decimated by what he read. His abuse of prescribed medication. His violent temper. His lack of accountability. All this and more was revealed in this memoir entitled, *Elvis: What Happened?* On more than one occasion, after reading the galleys, he said in a tortured way to those of us who were there, "My life is over." The book was released just ten days before he died. He knew the effects this book would have with the media and the public.

Elvis's dark private self was exposed. His deepest fear had come true.

Had Elvis recognized, admitted, and exposed his transgressions himself, I believe he would be alive today. So isolated was he from the reality of his own condition, he could see neither his problem nor his solution.

Imagine if Elvis had stepped forth and said, "Friends, I need your help. I have a problem. Pray for me. Help me get through this." I know it's hard to conceive, but I personally feel that had Elvis done that, he would have been even bigger today than he already was and continues to be.

The model that guided his life, the one he had passed on to me from the very beginning, "Deny everything," ultimately led to his demise.

I am sure you have had role models who taught you what to do *and* what *not* to do. And role models whose lessons took you years to understand and embrace. This was my experience with Elvis. It would not be until the end of my evangelical period that I embraced the fatal cost of isolation and began to instead choose the lifesaving benefits of transparency.

This was perhaps the most valuable lesson I ever learned from Elvis. One that continues to serve me well.

For Elvis to be as complete a teacher as he really was, and continues to be to me personally, it is necessary to look as closely at the dark as to the light. To only focus on Elvis's extraordinary gifts is to deprive ourselves of half of the teacher that Elvis in truth was. He not only illuminated a bridge from conventional dogma-based religion to expansive spirituality, he also illuminated the dangers of not reconciling our public image with our true self. As well as not dealing with the darker sides of us that sabotage our ability to embody our authentic spiritual self.

Questions to Ponder...

Lack of trust creates isolation. Isolation keeps us from being all we can truly be. It creates fear and uncertainty. It produces lack of confidence, which puts you in a position to miss so much of your own greatness and so much of the love that surrounds you. Ignoring your isolation and your darker sides can drive you further into darkness. It can create arrogance because when we're isolated we don't know what we don't know. It can cause one to fall into an affair as a way of protecting ourselves from fully opening our heart to the one we really love. Overeating, drinking, doing drugs, or any other form of anesthesia can be a direct result of isolation.

To truly step into the fully illuminated spiritual path of self-realization one must develop the habit of living in transparency.

- What parts of your life, or your inner self, have you isolated from the world?
- What fears do you have about what might happen if you were to move into more complete transparency?
- What would it take for you to step more fully into transparency?

Perhaps the most important lesson I can offer to anyone reading the pages of this book is to get out of the glass house that you've created. Go inward and be honest with yourself. Identify all the things that have driven you into isolation, and measure the devastating results that this isolation has cost you.

True spiritual enlightenment can only be achieved when we allow the light of the true authentic spirit that lives within us all to drive out the darkness that seeks to destroy us.

The cure is transparency. First with yourself, then with others.

CHAPTER EIGHT

THE TEACHABLE SPIRIT

My confession to Kandis, my pastor, and the church congregation had been my biggest shift from isolation to transparency, up to that point in my life. My transparency opened the door for my teachable spirit to begin to thrive. Yes, I still believed, but what did I believe?

While this was a step in the right direction, so instilled was the dogmatic denominational doctrine of my mother's church that I still felt incomplete. In my corporate talks I wasn't preaching to a congregation but I continued to inject my fundamental core beliefs within the structure of my keynotes. While this sustained me as a speaker there remained an emptiness and an unexplained fear in my life because I still hadn't made sense of the miracles I saw with Elvis.

The closest I came to these miracles is when I spoke at Assembly of God churches during my evangelism years. This was the denomination in which Elvis was raised. In that place they believed in the laying on of hands and praying for healing. I remember the first night I called the congregation who were in need of physical and emotional healing to the altar.

Like Elvis had done with me so many years before, I laid my hands on many and prayed in the name of Jesus Christ that they would be healed. Many were. Through all of it, I always knew that it was the power of God working through me as one of His servants.

When I said, "I still believe," that meant I believed the Bible. There is an old expression that says, "God said it, I believe it, and that's it." It goes on to say, "God said it and whether I believe it or not, that's it." There's one thing for certain. At that time I believed in the infallible, inerrant word of God.

Despite what I was experiencing in the Assembly of God and the gifts I'd seen in Elvis, in many of those churches there was still a judgmental, condemning approach to salvation. Nevertheless, the healings that I was part of in these churches challenged the beliefs I had acquired from my mother's denomination. Even though my faith increased as I witnessed the miracles of God in these churches, I was still very much in fear, so instilled in me were the dogmatic dos and don'ts that contradicted the beliefs I had from my youth.

Being part of those healings simultaneously reinforced my faith and challenged my dogmatic beliefs. This challenge matured me and brought my teachable spirit to a new level. It also gave me a better understanding of the miracles I had experienced with Elvis.

What I liked about the church was the teachings and miracles I witnessed through my study of the Word of God and the teachings of Jesus Christ. That has never been an issue in my life. What I didn't like was the idea that if you weren't like us or you didn't embrace our dogma you were going to hell. I just didn't like the rules, regulations, and rituals of these denominations.

What resonated in my soul were the words, "God so loved the world...." To me this didn't mean parts of the world, or one people but not another, or one denomination over another, or one religion being better than another. It meant the entire world. It didn't mean whites but not blacks, straights but not gays, Christians but not Buddhists, Republicans but not Democrats, or Americans but not Pakistanis. For me, "the world" meant the entire world.

But like many of you who grew up in a similar situation to mine, we simply didn't know how to adopt a broader worldview without disappointing the deacons and family members who had nurtured our early spiritual development. Then there was the question of what to do with the fear that maybe they were right that only some people got to God. For most of my life, this has been my challenge.

My years in the ministry didn't resolve this for me. Eventually, I left that world of speaking altogether. For, you see, on the road throughout the

'80s and '90s and into the new millennium I saw too many great, wonderful, loving people who I couldn't mark as doomed because they didn't share my fundamental core beliefs. During this time I continued to go to church on a regular basis. But, each time the pastor spoke, with every fiber of my being I was disgusted whenever it got down to it being his way or no way. Somewhere between what God taught in the Word and what Elvis taught me as a mystic and healer, lay the truth. It was this truth that I began to truly thirst for.

Ironically, this search kept me isolated. So strong were my convictions that God loves us all that I could no longer associate with any church or denomination that did not embrace the true and all-encompassing breadth of God's love. I was now in the wilderness somewhere between what others believed God said and what God meant.

Many of you reading this book are in this wilderness, too. You know those feelings of abandonment, isolation, and non-belonging. And the only way to deal with it, my friends, is very simple. It is to do what I suggested in the last chapter: become transparent, not only with your transgressions, but with that still, small voice that says, "Be still and know that I am God."

For me, this was the first step in my spiritual journey and path to enlightenment. Shedding the limiting ideologies and methodologies that we are programmed to believe is one of the most difficult steps in opening up to our teachable spirit. This involves the one thing that I had never been able to do in my life. The one inconceivable act that I could never bring myself to do. Trust.

Trust in your own heart. Trust in your own God-given gift of discernment. Trust in Him sending you the angels that will help you. Some you've ignored, some you've seen, and some are yet to come.

My first angels were my mother and Vernon, who unbeknownst to them put me in a place where I would be taught by a master. My second angel was that master, Elvis Presley. It was he who challenged me to think outside the box, outside the boundaries of fundamentalist philosophy and traditional religion. He not only taught me this, he showed me this.

Elvis used to sit in a room, look at the wall, and have conversations with his twin brother who had died at birth. I overheard him saying things to him like, "Tell Mom I love her and miss her." This showed me the depth of his belief in life after death. Witnessing him do this made it easier for me to trust my own experience when Elvis started coming to me after he died.

Yet, I didn't know how to handle this because my teacher of spirituality had died as a result of his human frailties. Which was I supposed to trust? His spiritual wisdom hadn't saved his life, so was I supposed to continue to be his apprentice or was I supposed to believe that he was a false prophet and only the God of my mother's church could save me?

This is the dilemma I struggled with throughout my life from the time Elvis died. Throughout the '90s and well into the new millennium, I continued to make a series of self-destructive decisions that not only hurt me but many of those around me. I did this because I wasn't fully able to trust Elvis as my angel, so that I could fully embrace the lessons he had imparted to me when he was alive. This is why I was so angry with him. All that kept me going was his promise that I would see him in a different place on a higher plane.

As vague as this sounded to me at the time, I also knew that I would in fact see him again. Yes, I would see him in dreams, and I would wake up to have conversations with him. Although we didn't have a connection in which it felt like he was still teaching me. It was as though he was waiting for me to start applying the lessons he had taught me. What I didn't understand at the time was that this could not happen until I abandoned most of the dogmatic teachings of my mother's church that I had learned as a child.

I spent so many years in the wilderness because I was in the midst of an inner battle between wanting to fully embody Elvis's teachings and fearing the spiritual and social consequences if I did.

I quit speaking as my primary job in early 2000. Although I recognized the fact that I had been gifted as a speaker, I no longer felt like my speaking was having the effect that I felt it was meant to have. At this time I didn't know what I believed. I changed careers and started a company called Impello Films.

I wrote, produced, and directed a story about my life with Elvis called *Protecting the King*. I had raised millions of dollars to make this film a reality. In the film I depicted my life with Elvis as accurately as possible. The most difficult scenes for me to recreate and direct were the last time I saw him alive and the death scene. During the filming of these scenes I often told my co-producer, Scott Vandiver, that we're doing this for a reason.

It was my first feature film and there we were, reenacting one of the most influential events in the history of pop culture. While doing this, I felt his presence like I hadn't since the last time I had seen him alive. Of all the scenes in the film, this is the most realistic and haunting. Elvis was saying goodbye to me again for the last time. I was again rushing up the steps and into his bathroom to discover his lifeless body. Scott reminded me that this was happening for a reason. That Elvis had something he wanted to share with the world, and he had chosen me to share it with.

Again, blinded by the realities of his death, I was unable to embrace this reality of the spiritual lessons he had shared with me during his life. In making this picture my self-destructive tendencies increased dramatically. I was eating more and drinking more than I had ever done. My weight ballooned to 320 pounds. My inward isolation was having devastating effects on me.

But, even through this wilderness I still believed. I still believed that Elvis would show me the way. I still believed he had something for me to share. I still believed that there was a new angel on the horizon. And I still believed that this angel would be presented to me.

Upon completion of the film, I needed to get releases from individuals who had been depicted in it, including my first wife, Angie. I had not talked with her in almost thirty years. When I called her to ask if she would be willing to sign off on the film, she said, "Sure. Send me the paperwork."

Rather than send it, I decided to take it to her personally. We met at a restaurant in Nashville. She told me what she thought of the rough cut of the film that I had sent her prior to coming. I laughed when she said, "David, I wish I had looked as good as the girl who played me."

I warmly reminded her that I had always thought she was beautiful. We talked about old times, and how we were mere kids when we first met, and how even though our marriage hadn't worked, we sure had a lot of fond memories. After she signed the paperwork she took my hand. I felt something between her palm and mine. "I accidentally took this when I left thirty years ago. I remembered I had it because the character who played you in the movie wore one of these throughout the entire film. I think it's time for you to have the real one back."

When I opened my hand, there was the ankh that Elvis had given me so many years ago when he initiated me as his young apprentice. I was instantly filled with his presence.

The film was released in 2007 and was distributed all over the world. Letters and e-mails began to flow in as fans asked me, "What do you think he meant when he said 'I'll see you in a different place on a higher plane?'" The answers began to come to me. It was time for me to share that message.

But I just couldn't do it. The timing just wasn't right. I hadn't yet found the courage to stand and proclaim that all I had been taught as a kid about God, about faith, and about organized religion was not enough, and that there had to be more.

I initially sensed what that "more" might be during a production meeting in Los Angeles in 2005. I had just had a chiropractic adjustment from my friend Dr. Richard Kaye. When I got up from the session I surprised myself as I asked him, "Can I tell you about Elvis and who he really was?"

This puzzled Richard. Of course he, like most, knew of Elvis the legend, but he had no idea what I was about to reveal. His curiosity was peaked. "Certainly," he said.

I settled into a chair, feeling a part of myself that I had denied for so many years. I felt inspired, as though the time had come to be more transparent about my life with Elvis than I had ever before been.

For how many hours I cannot recall, I told Richard about Elvis the healer, the mystic, the wonderfully generous human being he was. I shared with him how he parted clouds, how he moved the rainstorm so we could drive with our sunroof open, and how he was blessed with the gift of healing. Stories of "The King" unknown to many of those who cherished the music and the myth, poured forth from me for the first time.

It was in those moments that I first came to the conclusion that I needed to write this book. I realized that the truth must be told about who Elvis really was, beyond the façade, beyond the myth.

I wasn't ready. I first needed to broaden my teachable spirit in order to find peace in God. I needed to eliminate the illusions I had created in my personal life. And I needed to step into the greatness of my authentic self.

Questions to Ponder...

- Have you experienced or witnessed any extraordinary healings? If so, what impact did this have on your worldview? If you haven't yet, how might such an experience challenge your worldview?
- On a scale from zero to ten, rate how comfortable you are with your own spiritual path.
- On a scale from zero to ten, rate how comfortable you are with not needing others to believe as you do.
- On a scale from zero to ten, rate the extent to which you believe that unless others believe as you do they will go to hell.
- Recall the most powerful "spiritual wilderness" experience you have lived through. What was the epiphany this experience ultimately led you to?
- Who have your angels been? How have they been angels to you?
- Have you had contact with someone you've loved after they died? If so, how has this changed your worldview? If you haven't yet, how might this experience alter your worldview?

- Was there ever someone in your life who you didn't forgive for having died? What prices did you pay because of not forgiving them? If you did ultimately forgive them, what gifts did you harvest as a result?

- Do you have a remarkable story that you've not yet told to all those who might benefit from hearing it? If so, what is that story, what valuable life lessons does it contain, and who might benefit from hearing it?

CHAPTER NINE

EMBRACING THE GIFT

I wasn't quite ready to write the book that Dr. Richard Kaye and I had discussed. My journey kept bringing me face-to-face with the unanswered spiritual questions that I'd been asking myself from my early days as the young apprentice. My spiritual evolution wasn't quite ready to do this. There were still so many unanswered questions.

Questions like: why was I put into Elvis Presley's life? Why had it been me to whom he had exposed so much of his mysticism and healing gifts? Why had he said just two days before he died, "I will see you in a different place on a higher plane?" All of these questions, coupled with the ongoing conflict between my traditional faith and his metaphysics, still weighed heavily on my heart. This was on top of the disappointments I had experienced and the façade I had created in my world of evangelism.

Despite my transgressions, I was given a gift. The question that remained was why. As I got older, now in my fifties, I was rapidly approaching the time in my life when I could no longer put off my need to reconcile these two worlds of mine so I could embrace the gift that God intended for me.

"No man can serve two masters, for he will love one and hate the other."
~ Matthew 6:24

The inner struggle I faced was at times unbearable. It seemed that the closer I got to my understanding of God the more self-destructive I became. The Bible says, "No man can serve two masters, for he will love one and hate the other." It was time for a transformation.

Of all the fears I had experienced in my life, the one I had of missing the gift God had for me was the biggest fear of all. I've always believed that God has put in each and every one of us a gift. If there is sin in the world, and I believe there is, then that sin would be to have that gift but not recognize or use it.

As a speaker, one of my topics has always been "There's No Plan B." Plan B was making excuses not to step into and live in your Plan A, which, in my opinion, is your true authentic self. Much like Elvis, by this point in my life I had everything I had ever wanted. A beautiful home, a lovely wife, and a successful business. Even so, there remained a restlessness, a sense that I was still missing something.

My mindset after the release of *Protecting the King* in 2007 was to tackle this restlessness. My first attempts were unsuccessful. Rather than becoming introspective about all this, I instead once again found myself falling back into the old patterns. Patterns that were a direct result of my isolation that I had adopted throughout the years. As always, these habits hurt not only me but others around me, including my wife, Lynn.

Lynn and I had married in 1997. The best word I can use to capture her essence is "saint." This was a woman who not only embraced but also embodied the very essence of God's Word as a conservative Christian. She was sweet, kind, loving, merciful, and graceful. But her biggest gift was her extraordinary capacity for nurturing. Her life was devoted to nurturing others. I loved who she was, what she represented, and how aligned her life was with her religious beliefs.

She never judged me no matter what I did. In fact, it was Lynn who always encouraged me to seek what was right for me. But, even with all her love and nurturing, I became perhaps the most rebellious I had been in my entire life. I stopped caring about anyone or anything.

Still, my teachable spirit remained, and the still, small voice within me continued to whisper, "God has a plan for you." Through the example I saw in Lynn and the desire I had to discover God's plan, I made the decision to reexamine traditional Christianity. I was determined to choose, once and for all, what I authentically believed.

Being torn between two sets of beliefs, Lynn's authentic conservative Christianity and Elvis's authentic mysticism, was no longer tolerable to me.

I already knew that the fear-based "get right with God or go to hell" messages of my past could no longer be a part of my future. I also knew that the hedonistic it's-all-about-me mentality of so many misguided new-agers couldn't be a part of my future either. There had to be a balance.

A student of the Bible, having studied New and Old Testament theology while in college, I delved back into the Scriptures where I felt I'd find all the answers I still sought. I developed a liking for televangelist Joel Osteen. His preaching and his massive bestseller, *Your Best Life Now: Seven Steps to Living at Your Full Potential* was neither judgmental nor condemning. Rick Warren's *Purpose Driven Life* was another one of my favorites during that time as well. But, while I found these books less dogmatic than ones I had been exposed to before, to me they still perpetuated the message of "it's their way or no way." It was only more subtle.

In order to fully step into my calling I needed to resolve this religious dilemma that had been tearing me apart my whole life. As I started peeling back the layers of that dilemma, the lessons I had learned as a young apprentice came front and center.

I asked the God that is in all of us to teach me how to pray and how to meditate. I asked the God within all of us to reveal Himself, His message, and His mission for my life in a deeper way. In essence, I started over.

But, I could no longer accept that the conservative version of Christianity was the only way. My teachable spirit now began to expand to a higher level, opening me up even more. I no longer wanted mere Christianity. I wanted God.

It was at that time that I made the decision to fully rely on the central theme of the book, *The Impersonal Life*, which Elvis had given me so many years ago. It was time to embrace and act on its simple words at a level I had not yet done: "Be still and know that I am God."

One night, the miracle happened. God revealed Himself to me. An inner spiritual enlightenment came over me, the likes of which I had never before experienced. His light illuminated from within me. Anger was replaced with forgiveness. Prejudice was replaced with acceptance. Fear was replaced with love. And ambition was replaced with meaning. I embraced it all. The hole in my spirit was now being filled with the true essence of God.

The transformation I had so desperately sought for so many years had now taken flight. Gone at last was my isolation that had created my grand facade. For, you see, in that moment, I realized that I had been desperate enough for acceptance and love from other people that I had chosen to believe what they believed. Until now, I had chosen to do this instead of embracing what I knew in my own heart to be true about the very essence of God.

This revelation brought me to the conclusion that the key to God wasn't other people or outward dogmas, but rather in myself, and through the

God that lives within me. No longer would I look to other people for inner answers. Not to pastors, not to religious organizations, but to God Himself.

With this realization, my teachable spirit manifested into its fullest expression. Of all the gifts that Elvis had given to me during my life with him, it was his recognition and nurturing of my teachable spirit that had ultimately opened up the inner relationship with God that I had so desperately sought for so long. This was at last the higher place and different plane that Elvis had told me he would next see me in during our final conversation before his departure.

This is the place where I had not only found God but where I reconnected with Elvis, too. I had finally reconciled the parts of conservative Christianity that I still believed in with the mysticism that I experienced with Elvis as his young apprentice. In that moment it hit me that this was not only his gift to me, but his message to the world as well. And he had given it to me to bring to the world. This is how the apprentice had become the master.

The time had come for me to embody the greatness of my true authentic self. As well as to communicate this message that I believe is capable of transcending all religions and faiths, and unifying them in a way that can finally create the peace on earth that Christ called for.

Since then, the authentic spiritual David has, and continues to, steadily emerge.

The surrealistic, inauthentic world I grew up in had to die within me so it could be replaced with authenticity. I had just completed the most extraordinary journey of my life thus far. Doing this necessitated that I leave behind many people and beliefs that I had for so long been loyal to. This is the price of transformation.

While writing the pages of this book with my dear friend and colleague, Dr. Gruder, he pointed out to me that I had been on what is known as "The Hero's Journey" for the better part of my life. As a filmmaker, this was something I instantly understood. I had loved J.R.R. Tolkien's *The Hobbit* and *The Lord of the Rings*. He had brought the ancient archetypal hero's journey into today's world when he published his classics. At the same time during the early twentieth century, the revered Christian mystic C.S. Lewis published another hero's journey book series: *The Chronicles of Narnia*. I loved the films that were later made from these books. And of course I also loved George Lucas's *Star Wars* series, which he, too, had modeled after the classic hero's journey.

Dr. Gruder and I discussed how Elvis was obviously on a hero's journey, as was I. We also discussed how many millions of other people are drawn to these films because of the spiritual journeys they are on themselves. Perhaps even you.

The hero's journey begins with a seemingly ordinary person receiving a call to go on an adventure. Not just any adventure, but one with a very important purpose having to do with righting wrongs in the world and answering the call of God. Often, the invitation to embark on this journey is issued by one of the people who will become a main mentor or guide during the journey.

The hero usually rejects this call in the beginning; sometimes numerous times. We do this for three very important reasons. First, if we accept the call, we will leave behind the comfort of everything that has been familiar to us throughout our entire life. Second, we sense or know that to embark on an adventure this perilous might kill us. Third, we intuit that going on this journey will mean returning as a completely transformed person with a profoundly changed view of the world, and in ways we can't begin to envision.

The decision to embark on our hero's journey is the biggest one we have made, up to that point in our life. Once we leave our familiar world, we encounter unexpected guides and teachers who try to help us along the way. In spite of these, we often lose our way because of our own ego and inner misgivings. We usually come close to death, or what inwardly feels like death, on numerous occasions. And, most of all, we feel in the dark most of the time about how to proceed, and even about where our journey will ultimately take us. All we have in these darkest moments is a deep sense of purpose, even when that purpose is not yet fully defined.

If we successfully complete our journey we return home a completely changed person. We humbly realize that we are in fact no ordinary person after all, but that we have instead become fully authentic and have developed a deep sense of life purpose and calling.

We have grown far wiser because we now have a worldview and a range of life experiences that are far beyond almost everyone else in the village in which we grew up. Usually, we have become deeply spiritual and have evolved into being a mystic. And we have come to embrace how love is the most important thing of all.

Often, a time comes when a returned hero feels compelled to permanently move elsewhere to be among others who also have developed broader understandings because of their own journeys. And, just as they had guides and mentors on their own journey, sometimes these returned heroes become mentors and guides to others who embark on their journeys.

Listening to Dr. Gruder as he explained this to me, I came to realize that the scriptural saying, "Many are called; few choose" also refers to the hero's journey. (See Matthew 22:14.) When I began mine, I did not have the advantage of understanding the benefits of this ancient-yet-timeless road map that is so deeply ingrained in the fabric of humanity. Despite this, I intuitively took this journey, not yet knowing that this would lead me to the story of my life.

Like so many, I grew up an innocent child. Yet, that innocence was lost the first day I went on tour with Elvis in 1972. So huge was the gulf between my life on the road and my religious upbringing that I was always trying to put the genie back in the bottle.

In my attempts to do this I would develop a relationship with anyone I felt was pure. This was usually whoever my wife was at the time. The price of this way of life was that it split me into the three very different selves that we have explored previously.

There was the darker David who was fascinated with exploring the worldly perks of the road. There was the David at home who was trying to fill the role of a good husband and provider while hiding from my dark self. And there was the David who was always trying to embrace my authentic self through the spiritual lessons being instilled in me by Elvis, while also trying to not leave behind the fundamental lessons I had learned from my dogmatic Christian upbringing.

My incomplete hero's journey had dictated the rhythm of my life until the massive life-changing epiphany occurred that I described earlier in this chapter. As the apprentice who had now become the master, the time had come for me to fulfill the mission this had prepared me for. This called for courage and life-altering decisions.

Questions to Ponder…

- Are you caught between dogmatic religion and mysticism?
- Do you find yourself doing the same thing over and over, but getting the same results?
- Do you feel that you have been called or chosen?
- Do you have someone you trust and can be accountable to?
- What lessons have you learned so far from your hero's journey?

CHAPTER TEN

WALKING THE LABYRINTH

With the epiphany and transformation that had just taken place, I now needed to find the courage to leave the facade-laden relationship I had been in with one of the sweetest, kindest people I had ever known. While the evangelists of the '80s sickened me with their condemning, judgmental approach to Christianity, she personified to me what Christianity was truly meant to be.

I realize that the transparency I am revealing in telling this part of the story might be difficult to accept by some who read this. But, if one is going to allow God to illuminate the transgressions of his or her life, one must understand that while we can hide these transgressions from each other, it's His illuminated light that we cannot ignore.

Even though my journey was personal, until now I had been living my life out of fear of what others might think or say. Yet, at the end of the day, the only authoritative presence that any of us will answer to is God Himself. Much of the Christianity side of my life still resonated deeply for me, as it continues to, to this day. What had changed for me was that, at last, it no longer mattered what anyone else thought about my beliefs.

I knew it wouldn't be easy stepping away from my thirteen-year-long marriage. However, my transformation was real and my hero's journey had by then been completed. The result was that I could no longer live the facade-laden life I had created over the years. The next part of my journey not only meant walking away from the security of this marriage, but replacing the anesthetics that accompanied my life as a result of my self-imposed isolation.

This required courage and, for me, courage required trust. This newly found revelation would be among the most difficult challenges to emerge from my epiphany. Much like Larry Geller became Elvis's usher into the world of mysticism, I was about to meet mine.

I first came across Katy Manna on Facebook. She was a member of CEO Space, an international business development organization which I have been an instructor for since 2002. An organization with tens of thousands of members, I had last attended CEO Space in 2008. When my dear friend and founder of CEO Space, BJ Dohrmann, called me to come back and do a series of CEO Space previews throughout the country, and teach at the July 2010 Forum, I accepted.

Katy, an intuitive healer who attended her first CEO Space Forum in May of 2010, would also be at the July Forum. My first connection with her came through reading her daily "Live with the Lights On" posts on Facebook. Because of my epiphany, these posts had a profound effect on me. It was as though she was speaking directly to me. No words had touched me so deeply since my conversations with the King.

I knew I was meant to know her. Looking at her profile picture, I found her aura, charisma, and magnetism compelling. These qualities went far beyond her physical beauty. My epiphany had opened the door to my intuition, and my intuition said, "Write to her." I did. Her words resonated so deeply with me that the only words that came to me were, "Are you an angel?" She responded, "Yes, I am." I instantly had a trust in her that was completely new to me.

From that first text forward, I felt an energy from her. Her daily posts quickly became an important part of ushering me into the new world that was emerging within me. During my CEO Space Preview's summer tour, I found myself texting her to ask if she would send me energy before I stepped onto the platform to speak. Her energy was palpable to me each and every time, as though she was physically there. This, too, was a new experience for me.

I must admit that asking someone to send me their energy, and receiving it, was the first tree-hugging experience of my life. This was my first confirmation that Katy was indeed an angel sent from God to help usher me into a spiritual world that I had not experienced since Elvis passed.

As Katy recalls, "We met in person for the first time at a CEO Space Forum at which he was teaching, after about six weeks of private texts back and forth. I turned the corner to the lobby and saw him sitting there. He said, 'Katy Manna, I will never forget this moment.' We talked for hours.

"We were sitting on the sofa in his suite and our connection was undeniable. He was transparent. He shared the journey that he had recently completed that led him to his epiphany. He spoke of the dark corners of this journey, as though he wanted me to know who he had been and where he had come from. He didn't need to tell me. As an intuitive, I already knew.

"What kept playing in my mind and heart as we sat there and talked was, 'I'm just here to love you.' I know that's what he was feeling, too. As he shared things with me that he feared would make me run away, I embraced him and allowed him to be who he was, skeletons and all.

"He even warned me about getting close to him. I told him that I always go where I'm guided and that I had no doubt or fear, even though I also didn't have any idea myself about what was ahead for us. I only knew that I had been guided to him and we had come together for a reason.

"By the end of that Forum he changed his return plane tickets to stay longer because we could hardly bear the thought of parting ways. We both knew by then that God had something magnificent in store, and that destiny had brought us together for reasons yet to be fully discovered."

There were many reasons why I trusted that God had something magnificent in store. A particularly stunning one had to do with one of the first things I noticed about Katy. She had an ankh tattoo on her ankle. It is almost the exact same size and shape as the one Elvis had given me so many years before. The one Angie had inadvertently taken and had more recently given back to me during the filming of *Protecting the King*. Katy was deeply moved by how Elvis had presented me with the ankh, how it had subsequently been misplaced, and how Angie had so beautifully returned it to me. It was obvious to both Katy and me that Elvis had more to say to the master who had once been his young apprentice.

Upon returning to Dallas, Lynn picked me up from the airport. I didn't have to tell her what she already knew: that it was time for me to go. She reminded me how much she loved me and then in her typical loving way, told me she understood. That all she ever really wanted for me was the best. I told her that I wanted the same for her. And the best for her was for me to get out of her way and let her live her life, and continue her journey, as God had planned for her. With that, my thirteen-year-marriage ended. We remain dear friends to this day because we loved each other enough to let one another go, even though this was the hardest thing in the world for us to do.

This needed to happen in order for the real me to begin to emerge. That real me, as we discussed in the last chapter on the hero's journey, included the desire to leave behind parts of my past that did not serve me any longer. The 1 Corinthians 13:11 puts it this way: "When I was a child, I thought as a child, spoke as a child, and understood as a child. But when I became a man I put childish things away."

From the time I started working for Elvis until when I had this transformational experience, I had used anesthetics, including one-sided relationships, to cover up my inner conflicts and fill the emptiness in my heart and spirit. Now I was ready to move beyond this, not because of "should," but because my epiphany had begun to fill the hole in my soul with an inner experience of God. An experience that would make it possible for my authentic self to fully emerge at its highest level.

As with ending my marriage, this too wasn't going to be an easy process. I had been raised on rock. In that world, it was live fast and die young. I had seen far too many people over the years, in addition to Elvis, who had never confronted their self-destructiveness, despite having had enlightenment experiences.

My challenge was now to restructure my life so this would not happen to me. Katy helped me understand that my epiphany didn't magically mean that the residue from my past, and the self-destructive habits this had led to, suddenly vanished. The next step for me was to release myself from that residue and those habits.

Soon after I left Dallas, I moved to Baltimore where Katy provided me with a place to stay while I was doing research for my next film project. As I continued opening up to her she never told me that I needed to change. She just listened as I explained to her the things that I wanted to eliminate, and new things I wanted to do. This included the book I had discussed with Richard Kaye so many years ago.

I explained to her my apprenticeship to Elvis Presley, and how that apprenticeship had to be for a reason. I told her that in my new-found epiphany, this reason had become crystal clear. She listened intently as I described the events of those years and after. I spoke about Elvis the mystic, healer, and prophet. As an intuitive, she soaked it all in. She agreed. "Your mission is to write *Conversations with the King: Journals of a Young Apprentice.*" But she, like me, understood that there were many things I still had to let go of before I would be ready to do so.

We would get excited about the book, but my excitement was quickly eclipsed by my fear and lack of courage to write it. This fear caused me to revert back to what I knew best: isolation. This was disturbing to Katy and she understandably withdrew. She had seen and fallen for the David that I was reaching toward but had not yet fully actualized. For me, those four months in Baltimore soon became a time of such isolation that it was as though I was living in a foreign country. In retrospect, I put far too much on myself far too quickly. I had needed to spend time in my internal wilderness before I could spend any more time with Katy, let alone write a book.

As much as I loved being in her presence, I knew that I had to use caution because of my history of looking to others to save me from my past. I could not put myself in that position with her. We both knew that it was time for me to leave.

About a week prior to my departure from Baltimore, I received a phone call that my dear friend, Lamar Fike, had died. I had known him since 1958, when my mother first met Vernon. He, along with Red West, was one of

Elvis's lifelong friends. Both had accompanied him to Germany during his two years in the Army. Lamar was the patriarch of Elvis's inner circle.

After Elvis died, Lamar was never the same. While he became successful in his professional life, his own isolation and the self-destructiveness this led to had now caught up with him to cost him his own life, just as it had done with Elvis so many years before.

Like Elvis, Lamar was a father figure to me. The news of his death was devastating. His son Jamie called me to ask if I would preach at his funeral. I did. Lamar had chosen to be cremated and then buried.

As his ashes were poured into the ground outside Waco, Texas, the undertaker looked around at the small crowd to see who would be the first to take the shovel and place in the grave the first patch of dirt. Without hesitation I stepped forward, took the shovel, filled it with dirt, and poured it into the grave. In doing so, not only was I saying goodbye to my other father figure; I was saying goodbye to the same self-destructive tendencies that I had in common with him and Elvis.

The symbolism of this had a profound effect on me. Here was another reminder from God that it was time to bury the self-destructive parts of my past in order to fulfill my destiny.

I returned to Baltimore and packed up to leave. That morning before I left, I told Katy that in order to write this book and launch the new chapter of my speaking career, I needed to fully embody my message, not merely speak it.

All of my life I had relied more on having been Elvis's stepbrother than on my own true self. Now the time had come for me to rely on me, to stand fully on my own and embody the greatness of my true authentic self.

Doing this started with attending to my own self-care, becoming self-accountable, and honoring the gift of my intuition, on a whole new level. In other words, the time had come for me to become truly self-reliant for the first time in my life. So, instead of telling Katy what I was or wasn't going to do, I said to her, "I'm not going to tell you. I'm going to show you. You will see."

Standing in the driveway on that cold March morning saying goodbye to Katy brought tears to our eyes. I asked, "Do you think this is the last time we are going to see each other?"

Katy replied, "No way. I will see you in California." Just before I got into the car, I took her hand, as Angie had done with me several years before, placed the ankh in it, and said, "Make sure you give this back to me someday." With that, I gently kissed her and left.

My drive from the east coast to the west coast was my drive into the wilderness. Driving through the desert of New Mexico on the freeway that replaced Route 66, I recalled a story that Larry Geller had once shared with me.

He had been with Elvis on one of his many cross-country drives from Memphis to Los Angeles. On one of these occasions, as they traveled Route 66 through the desert, Elvis suddenly pulled over and began to cry uncontrollably. He had seen something in the clouds that spoke to him in a particularly powerful way. They got out of Elvis's custom Dodge motor home.

He pulled Larry close to him. And as Larry recounts in *Leaves of Elvis's Garden*, he proclaimed, "It's God! It's love. God is love, Larry. God is in me, in you, he's in everyone."

Elvis had experienced this epiphany in the very desert I was now driving through. As I thought of this story, I felt that God was speaking to me as well, guiding me through my inner wilderness, just as He had done with Elvis back in 1965. So powerful was Elvis's presence in that moment that I pulled over and texted Katy to tell her how real the story Larry told me had now become.

When I arrived in Los Angeles I moved in with yet another friend from my Elvis days. This was crazy. I felt that God was certainly trying to get my attention. Here was one more person who I had met almost forty years ago, returning to my life, and who was on the same downward spiral that Elvis and Lamar had traveled. I thought to myself, "Okay, God, I get it."

Shortly after moving to Los Angeles, I made my way to the March 2011 CEO Space Forum in Lake Las Vegas, Nevada. This was the first Forum of the last five that I was not accompanied by Katy. I missed her. I was on my own. I was down, uncertain, fearful. Yes, I knew what needed to be done, and yes I knew I could do it. But, like so many people, my fear of the unknown was having its effect on me.

I had moved to Los Angeles in order to focus more fully on my next film project, the one that I had been developing for several years and that had taken me to Baltimore. I was now at the next CEO Space Forum to move that project forward. I felt the weight of the world on my shoulders: the loss of my daily contact with Katy, the heaviness of Lamar's death, and the question of how I was going to live my future in alignment with my epiphany. I was in the wilderness, once again facing isolation. I felt that the decisions I was about to make would dictate the rest of my life.

Then God spoke to me: "Tell them, David. Tell the world your story. Tell them about the book. Stop waiting for things to change in your life. Trust me, David. Be still and know that I am God. Tell them. Tell them your story."

When I heard God's voice, I was sitting at a meal table prepared to do something different from that. I was about to hold up the poster for my next film project in order to invite the people at my meal table to a financial presentation concerning the film later that night.

Instead, I listened to God. I placed the poster back down on the table. I leaned forward on the edge of my seat and said, "I have a book I want to write. It's called *Conversations with the King: Journals of a Young Apprentice*. It's a book about my spiritual journey with my stepbrother Elvis Presley. A book that reveals to the world the Elvis that was the mystic, healer, and modern-day prophet." I asked them, "What do you think?"

Just as I feel that God used Lamar and my new Los Angeles roommate to remind me of the dire consequences of my not stepping into my true authentic self, He had placed at my table a group of intuitives. Every single one of them. That was it. They all said, "Whoa." There was Laura Miller, Dean

Fulford, and others, who just sat, listened, and wept as I described why this book needed to be written, and why I, as Elvis's stepbrother and apprentice, had been selected to tell the story. I felt the presence of God in Las Vegas that night more than I had felt in any church in America. I also came to the conclusion that it wasn't that I needed to get rid of the negative ideologies of my past; I needed to define my quest and to step into God's calling, by announcing my message.

Suddenly, in that moment, the real issue became clear to me. I had been struggling my whole life not because I had self-destructive tendencies. Those were only symptoms. On this night it was finally clear to me that my one and only problem was that I had spent my whole life running from the greatness of my authentic self, my life's meaning, and my readiness to not allow anything to interfere with God guiding me toward it.

The next day, I was walking down the hallway and ran into my dear intuitive friend, Eve Hogan. I told her about my book. She was overwhelmed with joy on my behalf.

She said, "How come you haven't done this before?"

"Because I had been holding on to so many unhelpful things from my past."

"David," she said, "do you know what a labyrinth is?"

"No."

She responded, "Well, come downstairs to the West garden later and I'll show you."

I did. I met her at the Labyrinth later that afternoon. She explained the ritual to me. Many hundreds of years old, labyrinths are inner simulations of outer pilgrimages. Most labyrinths today are modeled after the most famous one at Chartres Cathedral in France. In a meditative, prayerful, and intentional way, you walk the labyrinth's three-fold path: taking an inner journey to its center, remaining there for awhile in inward contemplation, and then walking out following that same path. Here is a bit of what Eve Hogan says about each of these parts of the labyrinth ritual in her book, *Way of the Winding Path: A Map for the Labyrinth of Life.*

The first part of the journey focuses on self-observation, contemplating our life circumstances and clearing the obstacles we discover as we walk. On a traditional pilgrimage the obstacles we must overcome are usually physical and external—difficult trails, heavy loads, and long distances. On the metaphorical journey within the labyrinth, the obstacles that must be cleared are internal—beliefs, perceived rules, emotions, memories, judgments, fear, grief, and ego, which once surpassed bring us to our own sacred center.

The center of the labyrinth, the heart, represents the sacred destination. Just as on an outward pilgrimage, you sit or stand in meditation open to receiving guidance or insight. Whether you receive an answer to a question, a valuable insight about your life, or merely a sense of peace, solitude, or joy, the center is a quiet space in which you get what you need. This might be what you thought you came for, or it might be different from that. Regardless, the center of the labyrinth provides the solitude necessary for accessing your inner wisdom and hearing the whisper of your heart.

The journey out of the labyrinth represents Divine Alignment—returning home, in union with God, to apply in your daily life the insights and wisdom you gained on your pilgrimage. This action step is critical for bringing about the transformation that extends beyond the pilgrimage to the transformation of your life toward wellness, wholeness, and health.

As you can see from this description, this symbolic ritual contains similar elements to the Hero's Journey that you read about earlier in this book. I took my first step into the labyrinth not yet realizing that in doing this I would solidify the gifts I received from that Hero's Journey.

Every curve I left something behind me. When I got to the center I opened my arms, lifted my head, and said, "God I am here."

"Be still, my son, and know that I am God," was the response I heard.

It was March 17 at 1:35 in the afternoon. I left it all in the center of that labyrinth. As I exited, standing there with open arms was Eve Hogan.

"Are you alright, David?"

I was overwhelmed with emotion and could barely speak. All I could say was, "I left it all right there in the center." I looked at my watch and said, "Eve, it's March 17 at 1:35 p.m. You just witnessed a miracle."

She saw how different I was when I came out of the labyrinth. I was glowing. She extended her arms and we hugged in celebration. During my time at the March Forum I was texting Katy about what was taking place. Despite the distance she remained supportive, saying that she was happy for me and encouraged me to keep going.

All of us make decisions about changing our life. But, what I had just experienced was more than a head change. I knew with every fiber of my being that this was a truly transformational heart change.

And it was. Everyone could see it. My inner transformation was now starting to be reflected in my outer demeanor. When I went back to Los Angeles I began working out, eating right, and I began to structure the outline of this book. I had never been as clear or on a mission as I now was. My life habits were now supporting my mission.

I called my friend Dr. Gruder, a fellow CEO Space instructor who I had first met at the September 2010 CEO Space Forum. Dr. Gruder is a psychologist and author who I was about to find out had been at Woodstock in 1969. He was an interesting character to say the least. During our first conversation I told him about my life with Elvis and the meaning I felt it had had. As he listened I wasn't sure if he was wearing the hat of a psychologist or an ex-rock-and-roller like me. But, what I did know is I liked him and felt that of all the people I had met in my life he was one of the few who could understand the implications of my life as a young apprentice to Elvis Presley.

I told Dr. Gruder that of all the people in the world, I am one of the few who has never been able to close the casket on Elvis because I felt that the huge world of Elvis fans wouldn't let me. He responded by saying, "I'm not sure you're so alone in this. It seems to me that there are millions of Elvis fans who haven't closed his casket either."

"Interesting. Why do you think that's so?"

Dr. Gruder's response was simple: "Because he has a message that people sense is there but they can't put their fingers on."

"Interesting you say that because I've had an idea for a book about this." As I explained to Dr. Gruder everything I felt was behind the book, he was intrigued. Then I told him the name of the book.

He responded by saying, "That's why you're Elvis's stepbrother. You're the messenger now, and that's what you've been carrying around all these years. You've got to write this book."

"Oh, yeah?" I replied. "Okay. If that be the case, then you're my co-author."

It was the case. I felt that I got a nod from God when Dr. Gruder revealed to me that his birth name was David Stanley Gruder.

That was September 2010 and it was now mid-March 2011. As a result of all that I left behind when I walked the labyrinth I was now ready to write this book, which I had first realized back in 2005 needed to be written. Now I had the clarity and courage to tell the story I have long felt the world needs to hear.

The massive inner shift I had undergone made changing my life habits natural and easy. I didn't have to use willpower to start eating differently and exercising daily. Quite the opposite. Doing anything other than that would have felt wrong to me. I was living from my inner self and my outer self was reaping the health benefits.

I stopped isolating and as a result my self-destructiveness naturally fell away from me. I replaced self-destructive habits with meditation and study.

I was no longer going to go it alone. A new aliveness was brewing inside me that was now ready to explode and pour out. As my confidence blossomed to a new level, the question remained, "What do I do with this power?"

I had always been a reader but my library now changed dramatically. It was becoming more metaphysical. The books I was now reading included *Entering the Castle* by Carolyn Myss, a book that Katy had ironically given to me months before, and *The Shift* by Dr. Wayne Dyer. I also returned to the metaphysical books I had seen Elvis reading, now embracing them myself from a completely changed perspective.

The next time I saw Katy, she saw a very different man. The man she fell in love with beneath the layers of self-destructiveness that I had not yet let go of. A man who now matched the potential she had seen when we first met. I was fully present, fifty pounds lighter, and embodying my authenticity more completely than ever before.

While it was clear to both of us that I had made strides, we both knew that it wasn't yet time to come back together. Back in L.A., I was busy laying the foundation that would birth this book. Dr. Gruder and I had started writing.

Questions to Ponder…

Virtually all of us have had our share of outside-the-box life experiences. There are only two ways we can respond to them. We can embrace these experiences and allow them to become God's gift to us. Few of us do this, however, because of how risky this is, since the shift this creates in our perspectives and choices can sometimes cause our life to change in unexpected ways. Or we can sidestep these gifts by clinging to our preconceptions and ideologies about ourselves, love, God, and how the world works.

- What outside-the-box life experiences have you had?
- Which of these two choices did you make with each of those experiences?
- Have you been leading an isolated life in which you'll die unless you shift into your authenticity?
- Have you been using the band-aid of self-medication to cope with your isolation?

If so, I encourage you to find the courage to replace your band-aids of self-medication with your authentic spiritual self, through self-realization. Allowing yourself to be transformed by outside-the-box life experiences is your doorway into this.

CHAPTER ELEVEN

THE PRICE OF INAUTHENTICITY

I had always known that my life had a purpose and that I had been placed at Graceland for a reason. I was committed to discovering and living that purpose. I trusted what Elvis had said about my having a teachable spirit. I had set out on my quest, which was to discover my life purpose.

The road was "long with many a winding turn," and filled with many discoveries I needed to make before I was ready to embrace and embody the greatness of my authentic self.

It would take me many years and much pain to discover that the habit of isolation, and the self-destructive habits it inevitably leads to, sabotaged my ability to succeed with my quest. Eventually, I was bludgeoned into surrender, as Dr. Gruder puts it. No one knew this because of how well-developed my sanitized public self had become. Only then was I ready to do something drastically different from what Elvis had done, so I could fulfill my commitment to not end up as he did.

My spiritual surrender made it possible for me to complete my hero's journey. This led to my epiphany, which opened me up to having my transformative labyrinth experience. This freed me to shed my isolation and enabled me to at last shed my self-destructive habits, which gave me access to the courage I had needed to fully embody the greatness of my authentic self.

The journey that began with Elvis so many years ago had at last led me to my life purpose. It made possible my metamorphosis from apprentice to master, and this opened in me the courage to write this book.

There is a saying that we teach best what we most need to learn. I didn't know it then but this is what I was doing in a new series of keynotes in 1990, which I titled "Solutionary Dynamics." The steps I taught were my variation on the universal, time-honored formula that has been worded in different ways by so many figures throughout history, and all the way to this day:

"Quest Definition plus Decision minus Fear plus Action plus Focus plus Quest Management equals Success."

My keynote is now "Embodying the Greatness of the True Authentic Self." The time-honored formula that I expressed through my Solutionary Dynamics programs helped guide me to the epiphany and ultimate transformation that led me to my true authentic self.

Quest Definition

After Elvis died I defined my quest in two ways: not ending up as he did, and finding out God's reason for why I had been dropped into Graceland and Elvis's world.

Decision

Despite how I defined my quest, I initially started heading down the path that had led to Elvis's demise. I, too, isolated myself and had no accountability, and nearly died twice back then as a result. That's when I decided to try God and entered the world of evangelism. But, it wasn't until I made the decision to find my true authentic self that the changes really began.

Fear

No matter what I tried, fear held me back. It kept me locked in my isolation and the self-destructive habits that accompanied it. It kept me imprisoned in going back and forth between trying to live in alignment with conservative Christian ideology and rebelling against it. Somehow, I kept moving forward bit by bit despite my fear. But, let there be no doubt that the fear that lived within me slowed my journey considerably.

Action

In time, the damage I did to myself and others because my fear was running my decisions accumulated to the point where I knew I needed to at last break through it or die trying. The time had come for a type of action I had not yet taken. That action was to break free from evangelism's ideologies and methodologies, and, later, from the world I had built around these. This action led me into the wilderness of the hero's journey. This ultimately led to my epiphany and to walking the labyrinth, using it as a ritual to shed the beliefs and patterns that I now knew stood between me and fully stepping into the greatness of my authentic spiritual self. This, in turn, made room for my teachable spirit to help me start trusting my intuition and shed the self-destructive habits that had kept me in the prison of isolation. I opened up to Katy and Dr. Gruder.

Focus

Now, clear at last about why Elvis had been put in my life and what my life purpose was, I became singularly focused on birthing this book and its message. I knew that doing this would create the foundation and platform for the rest of what I am called to do in my life, which is to bring this message to the world.

Quest Management

I devoted myself to replacing self-destructiveness with self-care, replacing isolation with transparency, and replacing fear with love. This was all part of managing my transformation, and it still continues to be. This book, and the management of my mindset and life today, is a direct result of successful quest management. *Conversations with the King: Journals of a Young Apprentice* marks the first step in my new quest, which is to bring to others the lessons I've learned and the wisdom I gained from completing my original quest.

The Risks, Prices & Gifts of Living Your Life as an Authentic Spiritual Self

Why do so few of us take the journey to our authentic spiritual self, and why do so many of us who do take so long to get there?

According to Dr. Gruder, the answer to both these questions has to do with risks we take when we step into the greatness of our authentic spiritual self. Some of those risks are real and some are imagined or fabricated. But, rarely do we know which is which until we have the advantage of looking back using the gift that twenty-twenty hindsight offers.

Personally, the risks for me had to do with stepping out of my comfort zone. It was easier for me to fall back on the certainty of my past than to have faith in the uncertainty of the future. That is no longer the case.

Even though I am now at peace with where I'm at in my spiritual life, I realize that some might not be. For example, my mother. How will she feel when she reads this? Then there are all the pastors, evangelists, and audiences I've worked with during my evangelical period. During the writing of this chapter I received an e-mail from an individual, asking what happened to me. He had heard me speak many years ago, told me I had been a powerful evangelist, and said he couldn't understand why I was dumping my Christianity. The truth is that I didn't dump my Christianity; I am simply no longer a prisoner of other people's expectations and ideologies. I now trust my direct inner experience of God and His guidance.

I realize that this fellow might be not alone. Some might be tempted to call this blasphemy. I simply call it the way God has guided me into developing a deeper relationship with Him. I am writing this to encourage people to believe as THEY authentically do in their own deepest heart and wisdom, regardless of the extent to which these beliefs do or don't match those of the people around them. I say this because I now experience the preciousness and sacredness of our inner experience of God. To me, this is far more important and real than believing what others think, feel, or say.

This illustrates one of the big risks of authenticity: being ostracized or rejected by some people who once felt close to us. It's one thing to risk being rejected by some people. It's another to risk being rejected by massive numbers of fans. Unfortunately, Elvis's lack of transparency was driven by the pressure he felt to be who his fans perceived him to be. I have often said that to love Elvis as I did, they would need to love him through all his ups and downs, joys and hurts, and self-destructive binges; not merely be in love with his talent, glamour, and stardom. Fact is, the world didn't know him. I did. And I loved him anyway. Unconditionally. So did God.

In the end, Elvis's lack of transparency cost him his life, as I've mentioned before. But, my ability to embrace it saved mine. For, you see, transparency in its truest form is the real author of authenticity. In truth, we all have intuition and it's not until we embrace and follow that intuition that we can truly learn for ourselves. I had allowed others to make my decisions for me by ignoring my own discernment and intuition. Letting go of this meant risking their disappointment and possibly their rejection.

Another risk was trust. In my world of evangelism and Christianity, I focused so much on finding the right person to trust that I missed the very essence of God's message. I felt that any trust I might develop with anyone outside of the world of dogmatic Christianity would be fatal to all that I held dear at that time in my life.

It was only when I met Katy that I truly dropped my guard. I've always been taught that trust is earned and oftentimes never deserved. In Katy I found a level of unconditional love that I was unaccustomed to, other than from God.

In our early communications, Katy just listened. As a result, the gift of her intuitive spirit cut through any of the defenses that I had created in my world of self-destructive isolation.

I have learned through my experiences with Katy that at the right time and the right moment God still sends angels. I believe that God does this to remind us that our relationship with Him is not through other people's beliefs but rather through our own inner experience. In addition, as in the case with Katy, love is unconditional, and the ones who truly love never expect anything in return, least of all allegiance to their ideologies.

Another risk was that if I let go of my preconceptions and facade-laden ideologies about life and God, I wouldn't know who I was. I would be adrift and lost. Dr. Gruder refers to this as Disorientation Fear. Paradoxically, we can't find God until we find the courage to survive this disorientation.

Disorientation fear blocks our connection with God. It is created by a conflict among the three selves that all of us have: our sanitized public self, our dark private self, and our authentic spiritual self.

When we choose to align with our authentic spiritual self we risk finding ourselves quite alone among so many others who still identify with their public self and are desperately trying to hide their dark self. For most of my life, I could be in a room full of people who love me and never feel love at all. I was always there in body. My sanitized public self was there. I was really good at letting people see the person I wanted them to.

Growing up with Elvis I became an expert at this. There was no accountability at Graceland. It was all about image management. Remember, it was Elvis who said, "The image is one thing. The man is very much different."

I was drawn to Dr. Gruder not only because he's a doctor of psychology but mostly because he specializes in integrity. I asked him, "What is the definition of integrity?"

"The dictionary defines integrity as a state of being whole and complete, and in alignment with some code of morals or ethics," he explained. He went on to say that the problem with this definition is, who decides what being whole and complete is, and which moral or ethical code are we using? He told me that the dictionary definition is "true but not useful."

In his long-time study of people who are sustainably happy, he found the definition of "whole and complete" that he was looking for. In his book, *The New IQ: How Integrity Intelligence Serves You, Your Relationships and*

Our World, he explains that the secret to sustainable happiness is living life at the intersection of the three core drives that all of us come into this life with: "Our drive to be who we truly are, our drive to bond with others, and our drive to influence the world around us. This translates into authenticity, connection, and impact." Dr. Gruder went on to share with me these three core drives form this "moral code of integrity" that we humans carry within us: Authenticity is self-integrity, connection is relationship integrity, and impact is societal or collective integrity. His point was that it's impossible to be happy without integrity and it's impossible to have integrity without being happy.

I replied that it sounded to me like he was describing our authentic spiritual self. He agreed wholeheartedly. I also said that he had just explained what happened to Elvis, and the influence this had on my life. While Elvis had been the most recognizable person to deal with this dilemma he is by far not the only one.

I said, "Dr. Gruder, what you call integrity, I call accountability. I have always said that Elvis's death was directly caused by the lack of accountability."

This reaffirmed that he was the guy to write this book with me. For, you see, the combination of where I had come from and what I had experienced, along with Dr. Gruder's expertise in integrity, was the glue that brought together as unlikely a team as the two of us.

Elvis was the healer, the mystic, the teacher. But, in the end, he missed the most powerful of all ingredients: accountability. The splits between his public self, his dark private self, and his true authenticity were so huge that I believe they tore him apart in ways that he never found a solution to. This dilemma has been shared by many celebrities, including Michael Jackson, who also became trapped in a world that lacks transparency. A world in which there is such a gap between their public image and their private self that they are often destroyed because they never discover what to do about this.

Hidden within the deaths of these two kings (Elvis and Michael) were secret signatures of salvation. Beneath the obvious prescription drug dependency and lack of transparency lived an irresolvable dilemma. Their massive talent could only express itself so far in the absence of transparency, and the gulf that this created in their soul seems to have become too much for them to bear.

Tolerating a split among our three selves is unsustainable. It's only a matter of time before our dark private self overwhelms and eclipses our sanitized public self and snuffs out our authentic spiritual self.

Throughout this book I've clearly illustrated the effect this had on me. My point in doing this is to show you that you don't have to travel this path. One doesn't have to be an Elvis or a Michael, or any other kind of superstar or public figure, to fall victim to such imbalance. Each one of us faces the possibility of falling into this trap every day of our life.

It is only because I now know how to avoid this that I became able to co-create and love in an entirely different way. It has become clear to me that the highest test for authentic selves is creating sustainable love, and the only way to develop a sustainable marriage is to divorce your inauthentic self. For me, this now expresses itself in its highest form with the angel who appeared in my life in the form of Katy. Ultimately, we discovered that the purpose we were brought together for was to be married.

In the next chapter we will provide you with the lessons and antidotes to embody your true spiritual authentic self. The journey continues.

Questions to Ponder...

Not fully stepping into your authenticity is a form of death because unless you become fully authentic you're living a form of living death anyway. You don't have to be physically dead to be dead.

"Be still and know that I am God," resonated not only with Elvis but also with me. I've come to the realization that God lives in every one of us and loves us unconditionally. All that one needs to do is to call upon Him from within. He's only a breath away. Having the courage to do this is where transformation begins.

- What prices have you paid because of a lack of accountability or lack of transparency?

  On a scale from zero to ten, how much does your image line up with the person you really are? In what parts of your life is the alignment the easiest and the most difficult? What steps are you willing to take to become more fully aligned throughout all parts of your life?

- Aligning with your authentic self requires teachability, courage, and accessing the spirit within.

  On a scale from zero to ten, rate your current level of teachability, your current level of courage to step into your authenticity, and the current level to which you trust your ability to access spirit. If any of these levels are below where you want them to be, create an action plan for further developing that ingredient.

- Identifying with your authentic self requires stepping into your greatness with humility, self-responsibility, and accountability.

  On a scale from zero to ten, rate your current level of humility, your current level of self-responsibility, and your current level of accountability. If any of these levels are below where you want them to be, create an action plan for further developing that ingredient.

CHAPTER TWELVE

LIFE IN A DIFFERENT PLACE ON A HIGHER PLANE

Today, I live in my true authentic self. It's not that I no longer struggle with old pulls toward my facade-laden past. It's that I no longer choose them. Thirty-four years after the death of my world-famous stepbrother I have harvested the teachings he meant for me to gain, which in turn has allowed me to close his casket once and for all.

In doing this, I understand now more than ever why so many millions of people are still deeply drawn to him. I believe they know that he has lessons for them, but until now they didn't know what those lessons were. It turns out that these lessons are for more than only Elvis fans. They are for everyone who values spiritual development and being fully authentic.

It took me decades following his death to fully unravel and make sense of what he was trying to teach me. Now that I have done this I know that this is what he would have wanted to teach the world if he had found a way to become transparent. The reason I was in his life was to fill that function for him. In doing so I have ceased to be his apprentice and have transformed into the master, the teacher.

For the millions who continue to follow Elvis, the message is simple: See beyond his music to his soul. And see beyond his soul to his lessons about what to do and what to avoid on the spiritual journey. Only then will you be free to take the real Elvis the rest of the way into your heart and be at peace with his death.

Imagine what would happen if every one of Elvis's followers stepped onto their path toward enlightenment as described in this book. These millions upon millions could become the catalysts for changing the world through the universal love that comes from an internal intuitive connection with God.

My message to the mystics who continue to evolve on their personal spiritual journey is take to heart the lessons you didn't realize Elvis was holding for you, too. For some, this means to stop allowing your lack of accountability and transparency to block you from illuminating the gifts that God has given to you personally. This means to courageously face your dark private self and to stop acting as though your public self is your authentic self. Instead, allow your authentic self to be your public self.

For others in the world of mysticism, this means to stop judging those whose spiritual path lies within conservative religious traditions, and embrace them as your brothers and sisters who simply have a different spiritual path from yours. And, similarly, for some who resonate with conservative religious traditions this means to stop judging the mystics for their internal relationship with God, simply because it often does not revolve around conventional dogma.

The last thing we need today is to continue to beat each other to death in the name of whose version of God is right and whose is wrong.

I personally feel that I was Elvis's apprentice in order to call both the traditionalists and the mystics to action. For, you see, Elvis's message, the one he instilled in me, not only embodies his authentic spirit, but that of Jesus Christ as well. This was the message that went far beyond the image of Elvis. This was the message that came from Elvis, the modern day mystic, healer, and prophet that many of you did not know him to be before reading this book.

What was this message? It has been embedded in all of the lessons I've shared with you throughout this book:

- **You have three selves: your sanitized public self, your private dark self, and your authentic spiritual self.**

Your sanitized public self is the image that you want others to see and believe. Our public self includes some authentic parts of us. It also conceals other parts of us behind a mask. This mask has been carefully designed to make us appear to be more flawless than virtually any human.

Your private dark self includes the parts of you that you decided were scary for you to face and/or threatening to others to see. It is all of the parts of you that your sanitized public self is supposed to conceal. The problem is that we can't kill off parts of our self. Aspects of our dark self express themselves sooner or later, directly or indirectly, mostly privately but sometimes publicly, and with or without our awareness, but almost always in ways that harm others and/or us. In psychology our private dark self is frequently called our shadow.

Your authentic spiritual self is your truest essence. It is the precious core of your being and the holder of your sacred life purpose. And it contains all of your considerable God-given gifts. Some of your authentic self has become woven into your public mask. Other aspects you reveal only to some of those who are closest to you. And yet other precious parts of you might be so secret that you don't even let yourself fully embrace them.

The heart of the spiritual journey is about facing and transforming the parts of us that we have tried to hide in our private dark self and replacing our sanitized public self with more and more of our authentic spiritual self. The spiritual journey is our journey toward transparency. Through this book you got an in-depth look at Elvis's and my three selves. And the exercises in this book have offered you ways to develop a more conscious and self-responsible relationship with your three selves.

- **Each of your selves has had powerful teachers.**

  In general, the world tends to promote, reward, and even idealize sanitized public selves. It tends to harshly judge and punish dark private selves. And it tends to be threatened by or jealous of authentic spiritual selves. Because of this, most of us quickly intuit as children that we need mentors to show us how to develop an effective sanitized public self, how to hide our private dark self, and how to cope with our authentic spiritual self.

  We all have had mentors. Some have shown us what to do, others have shown us what not to do, and most have been "mixed bags" that have shown us a combination of both. Sadly, too few of us have been blessed with mentors who knew how to effectively encourage us to step into the greatness of our authentic spiritual self. Just as sadly, most of us have had mentors who have encouraged us to create and identify with our sanitized public self and have insisted that we hide our dark private self. You've read in this book about the impacts that my mentors had on me, and you have been offered exercises to explore the impacts your own mentors have had on you.

- **Your three selves are in conflict.**

    Our three selves have conflicting purposes. The mission of our sanitized public self is to hide our dark private self and the aspects of our authentic spiritual self that we believe others can't handle. The mission of our dark private self is to find a way to get us to pay attention to and transform it into a valuable part of our community of self, and this doesn't please our sanitized public self one bit.

    On the other hand, our dark private self deeply resents the ways in which our sanitized public self tries to keep it hidden. This is what causes our dark private self to periodically rebel by overwhelming or sabotaging our sanitized public self. This conflict between our sanitized public self and our dark private self squelches our spiritual authenticity and is the source of all transgressions.

    The mission of our authentic spiritual self is to transparently live our life purpose, to transform the parts of us that have become imprisoned within our dark private self, and to replace our sanitized public self with our true and real self. This book has provided the most complete picture ever of the conflicts among Elvis's three selves and the impact this had on the conflict I experienced with my three selves and his. And it offered you exercises to help you illuminate the conflicts among yours.

- **Isolation is the enemy of authenticity.**

     The very existence of our sanitized public self guarantees that we will feel isolated because on some level we know we're not being fully authentic. Feeling like we need to hide our dark private self guarantees that we will feel isolated as well. And believing that it is not a good idea to fully embody the greatness of our authentic self guarantees that we will feel isolated because we're never fully ourselves even when surrounded by a room full of people.

     Paradoxically, remaining isolated keeps the conflict among our three selves locked in place. This is profoundly painful. As a result, we increasingly use anesthetics to numb the pain that our isolation creates. You saw in this book the prices that both Elvis and I paid for our isolation, and you had opportunities to do exercises to discover the prices you have paid for yours.

- **Self-destructiveness is really a desire to destroy your "false self."**

     Our authentic spiritual self is never self-destructive. It would never have any reason to be. However, we intuitively know that our sanitized public self and our dark private self are not who we really are. They are false selves that interfere with our authenticity. On some level we know that our spiritual evolution depends on freeing ourselves from the bondage and tyranny of these false selves. What we call self-destructiveness is in actuality three things:

1) The cover-ups our sanitized public self engages in to hide our dark private self and aspects of our authenticity;

2) The damaging ways our dark private self periodically acts up in an attempt to get our attention;

3) The anesthetics we use to try to cope with the tension and conflict among our three selves.

This book offered you opportunities to look at your own "false-self destructiveness" as you also read about how this played out in Elvis's and my lives.

- **Transparency in its truest form is the real author of authenticity.**

    Wearing a mask in order to hide parts of who we are and ignore parts of us that need to be transformed is the opposite of authenticity. We are less-than-transparent because authenticity is not without risk. However, the prices we pay for not being authentic are greater. This book has given you a detailed portrait of the prices of being inauthentic, the risks of becoming transparently authentic, and the huge gifts that make taking those risks worthwhile.

- **Having outside-the-box experiences is how you discover that spirit is far beyond what you think it is.**

    These experiences are God's way of inviting us to get out of our own way so we can step more fully into the greatness of our authentic spiritual self. They offer us an expanded vision of our own potential, of love, and of more spiritual ways of viewing our life experiences and how the world works. However, even though these experiences are priceless blessings from spirit, the majority of us try to avoid them.

Unfortunately, many people who do have outside-the-box life experiences like those described in this book tend to deny, disown, or distort them in order to remain loyal to their pre-existing beliefs. They don't allow these experiences to create the epiphanies that open the door to transformation.

Dr. Gruder refers to the addiction of clinging to our pre-existing beliefs despite having outside-the-box life experiences as Paradigm Attachment Disorder. I believe spirit means for us to grow throughout our entire lives. Your willingness to be transformed by outside-the-box life experiences is the biggest measure of your teachability. You saw in this book the extraordinary things that occurred because I had the courage to embrace these experiences and allow them to expand my vision, my beliefs, my authenticity, and my ability to love. Now it's your turn.

- **Paying a high enough price for not living from your authentic self is how you wake up.**

   Most of us get doctorates from the college of hard knocks. Unfortunately, most of us use those hard knocks to become more closed down, self-protected, hidden, and inauthentic. Dr. Gruder is particularly fond of this anonymous saying: "Mostly people change not because they see the light but because they feel the heat." It is up to each of us to decide how much heat we are willing to endure before we wake up. Each of us has free will about how high a price we are willing to pay before we unconditionally commit to going to any lengths to step into the greatness of our authentic self.

- **Accessing your authentic self requires replacing ambition with integrity.**

Our authentic self is not ambitious in the worldly sense of the word. Its ambition is to be whole, complete, and ethical. Its ambition is transparency, love, and positive impact in the world, in ways that honor our personal relationship with and expression of God. In other words, the focus of our authentic self is integrity not ambition.

Whenever we sacrifice our integrity for an ideology, a goal, or a worldly desire, we allow ambition to obliterate our authenticity. As Dr. Gruder says, we only sacrifice our integrity when we are pursuing a faulty happiness formula and don't know it. You saw in this book how Elvis's and my faulty happiness formulas backfired, and discovered how authenticity aligns our beliefs, goals, desires, and actions with integrity. Authenticity is the solution to the seemingly irresolvable conflict between our integrity and our happiness.

• **Aligning with your authentic self requires teachability, courage, and activating a strong internal connection with spirit.**

You have almost undoubtedly heard the saying that insanity is doing the same thing over and over expecting different results. The surefire way to keep doing the same thing over and over is to "keep our own counsel." Most people have used this time-honored phrase as a way to justify being impervious to influence from others whose world views differ from ours and to justify making ideologies, dogmas, and rules more holy than one's inner intuitive experience of God. In other words, too many people hide behind the notion of "keeping our own counsel" in order to make being unteachable seem like a virtue.

You've seen in this book how being unteachable is anything but a virtue, and how becoming authentic not only requires teachability, but courage and a strong internal connection with spirit as well. Developing this inner connection takes time, care, and persistence.

By all means give yourself full permission to question the parts of your existing beliefs that might be at odds with what feels true in your deepest self. At the same time, avoid the temptation to prematurely disavow your prior beliefs in favor of what might initially feel like intuition. Take time to carefully assess and reassess the various aspects of your faith. Don't throw out the baby with the bathwater. And always bear this in mind: learning to distinguish between your ego's voice, the things you wish—or fear—might be so, and accurately "hearing" your spiritually-guided intuition, is a discipline that requires great discernment to develop well.

- **Identifying with your authentic self means embodying your greatness.**

Those of you who have read Marianne Williamson's work may recall her famous quote from her book *A Return to Love*:

"Our deepest fear is not that we are inadequate. Our deepest fear is that we are powerful beyond measure. It is our light, not our darkness that most frightens us. We ask ourselves, who am I to be brilliant, gorgeous, talented, and fabulous? Actually, who are you not to be? You are a child of God. Your playing small does not serve the world. There is nothing enlightened about shrinking so that other people won't feel insecure around you. We are all meant to shine, as children do. We were born to make manifest the glory of God that is within us. It's not just in some of us; it's in everyone. And as we let our own light shine, we unconsciously give other people permission to do the same. As we are liberated from our own fear, our presence automatically liberates others."

You have read throughout *Conversations with the King* many examples of the prices that we pay for not fully embodying the greatness of our authentic self. You saw the ultimate price Elvis paid for having stopped short of fully embodying his greatness. You saw the many prices I have paid for having followed in his footsteps in this regard. My deepest wish and hope is that this book has inspired you to stop making the same mistake that Elvis did, and to instead join me in a commitment to embody the greatness of our authentic self. Not only for our own wellbeing. Not only for the sake of those we love. But for the sake of the world.

- **Living from your authentic self takes you to a different place on a higher plane.**

I can't begin to put into words how grateful I am to have finally joined Elvis in a different place, on a higher plane. The one he said he would next see me on in our final conversation just two days before he left his earth life.

He didn't get me there. Spirit did. And spirit only got me there because I was a teachable soul who ultimately found the courage to risk everything by setting aside my sanitized public self and transforming my dark private self so I could at last live my life from my authentic self.

I cannot think of a more sacred gift to offer to my master in gratitude for his having made me his apprentice. I cannot think of anything he would want more from his fans than for them to at last embrace these deepest messages and lessons of his life.

I also believe that my brother would be deeply gratified to know that the lessons in this book have helped other high profile public figures avoid the mistakes he made. And I know in my heart that he would be utterly delighted if this book offered valuable inspiration, encouragement, and lessons to those who are dedicated to their personal development.

In conclusion, I want to say one last time that I will always treasure my memory of the seventeen years I spent with Elvis. But, what I hold the most profound gratitude for was all that Elvis illuminated on my journey toward transformation. Both what to do and what not to do.

In the end, his death was my resurrection, his passing my wakeup call to my road to redemption. There is no question that he was the most influential person in my life, and the greatness I saw in him is the greatness that I have come to believe all can achieve by illuminating the realities that God has planned for each one of us.

The preface of this book began with perhaps one of the most profound questions I ever heard anyone ask of Elvis Presley: "Are you satisfied with the image you've established?" I now ask you this same question.

We've learned that Elvis was a highly spiritually evolved individual who only scratched the surface of his full potential. Is that you, too? I imagine that the answer is yes, to one extent or another. If so, I congratulate you. For, it is in this transparent state of mind, heart, and spirit that you have taken your next step toward embodying the greatness of your true authentic self.

About The Authors

David E. Stanley

David E. Stanley spent seventeen years growing up with his iconic stepbrother Elvis Presley. From 1960 to 1977 he was the young apprentice to an Elvis few knew—Elvis the mystic and healer.

Today, David Stanley is a bestselling author and filmmaker, and is a speaker in the field of self-development & authenticity.

His personal life story of triumph over adversity and stepping into greatness has impacted millions around the world. His powerful programs and contagious passion challenges and inspires individuals to embody the greatness of their true authentic selves.

David S. Gruder, PhD

Dr. David S. Gruder, PhD, DCEP, is a licensed clinical psychologist and award winning author & speaker in the area of self-development and spiritual growth.

Recognized as the foremost expert in the area of integrity, intentional effectiveness, and accountability, Dr. Gruder is a highly sought after speaker, who trains and consults with professionals, businesses, and leaders worldwide.

DAVID E. STANLEY SPEAKING ~ 2011
"EMBODY THE GREATNESS OF YOUR AUTHENTIC SELF"

SUGGESTED READING

The Impersonal Life/Joseph S. Benner

Leaves in Elvis's Garden: The Song of His Soul/Larry Geller

The Shift/Dr. Wayne Dyer

Enter the Castle/Caroline Myss

A Return to Love/Marianne Williamson's

The New IQ/Dr. David Gruder

Daily Manna: Your Guide to Life with the Lights on/Katy Stanley

Way of the Winding Path: A Map for the Labyrinth of Life/Eve Eschner Hogan